MONSTER DANCES AT DUSK

DURAIYA KHAN

Follow us @sacred.scribe.publishing
Tag us in your images #SacredScribePublishing
www.sacredscribepublishing.com

Monster Dances at Dust
Published by Sacred Scribe Publishing LLC
© Author, Text Duraiya Khan 2024
© Illustrations, Images 2024

Edited by Leah Shoman
Book Design and Artworks by Nuno Moreira, NM DESIGN
ISBN: 979-8-9879866-3-9
Printed and bound in China.

All rights reserved. No part of this publication may be reproduced or stored in a retrieval system or transmitted in any form or by any means electronic, mechanical, photocopying, recording or otherwise without the prior written permission of the publisher.

MONSTER DANCES AT DUSK

A HOLISTIC SELF-LOVE JOURNEY

DURAIYA KHAN

ACKNOWLEDGMENTS

Thank you to my London family for letting me spend a winter with them in a cozy home to explore my passion for writing.

Thank you to my Italian family for showing me il dolce far niente, helping me find my balance, and unlocking my creative potential.

Thank you to my Houston family who let me feel safe enough to share my story with the world.

Thank you to Morgan, Hanna, and Tiffany for staying by my side every step of the way and loving every version of me.

Thank you to Brooke for supporting me in my journey, proofreading my book, and encouraging me to go all the way in my storytelling.

CONTENTS

Beige Hour   7

Can't Breathe 11

Fish on the Moon   17

Subliminal Glitch   21

Uncovering the Trauma   27

Year Thirteen 33

Building my Pyramid   39

Caged Meadowlark   45

Hanged Doll 51

Saturn Return   55

Caught in the Seaweeds   61

Unlovable   65

Withering Away   69

Five of Cups 73

Mountains of Hope   77

Finding Enchantment   83

Luminescent Glow   89

Little Lion Strength   93

Queen of Pentacles   99

CONTENTS

Silver Ceremony   105
Skeletons in the Trenches   111
Mask Unveiled   117
Transcendence   123
Inner Child Speaks   129
Rebirth   133
Metamorphosis   137
High Priestess 141
Magician   145
Sea Dragons 149
Devil in Red Snakeskin 153
Emperor in Reverse   159
Empress State of Mind 165
Pearl Girl   171
Golden Hour 177

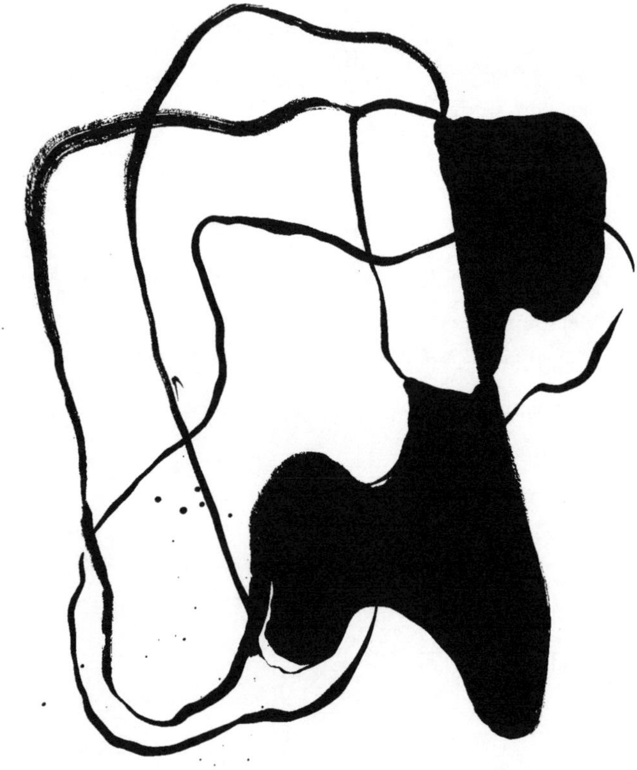

BEIGE HOUR

I'm in a field of mirrors planted in the ground like they
sprouted from seeds
Shattered and broken, growing amongst the dying beige weeds

Paper plane ticket in my hand with "one way" written on it
No bags, no plans, and I'm the only one standing at the gate

The airport terminal is empty and I'm roaming in ghostlore
Something feels so familiar like I've been here before

Sepia smoky skies obscure my surprise at this odd reminiscence
I start walking around slowly and make my way through the
scattered remnants

The large glass window is the only thing still there
Overgrown ivy climbing along it, no lights, no glare

My vintage blue airplane is parked beyond in the distant haze
A time machine waiting for me to get through this unusual maze

The jagged-edged mirrors are spaced out like gravestones of clear quartz
I walk by each one and look at my reflection, like looking into crystal balls of sorts

The visions change each time, the cracks and dust distort my face
I'm peering into other realms, perhaps stories of my past, or maybe into space

A different version of me each in a different time
My face is glowing in the moon, it's eerie and sublime
I'm not smiling or laughing, I just appear vacant in each scene
Recorded moments projected from my mind onto a smoke screen

A thousand pieces of a puzzle I can't seem to put together
Studying ripped-up pictures of my history in this foggy weather

I make it to the faded runway, but there's no pilot in sight
I'm abandoned, cold, and alone with all of these riddles tonight

Tangled grasses and thick pines of all the evergreen hues
Shades of emerald and jade, they kind of feel like clues

I suddenly wake up and I've returned to my lonely bedroom
I want to go back to the fields, I prefer to live in the gloom

Daydreams or nightmares, I'd rather be wandering through the castles in the air
Playing in alternate realities like spinning in teacups at the fair

The girl in my visions is always much more brave than me
She's wild and free, she isn't chained to this version of reality

I don't want to go back on auto-pilot, driving without purpose
But my alarm clock goes off and pulls me back to the surface

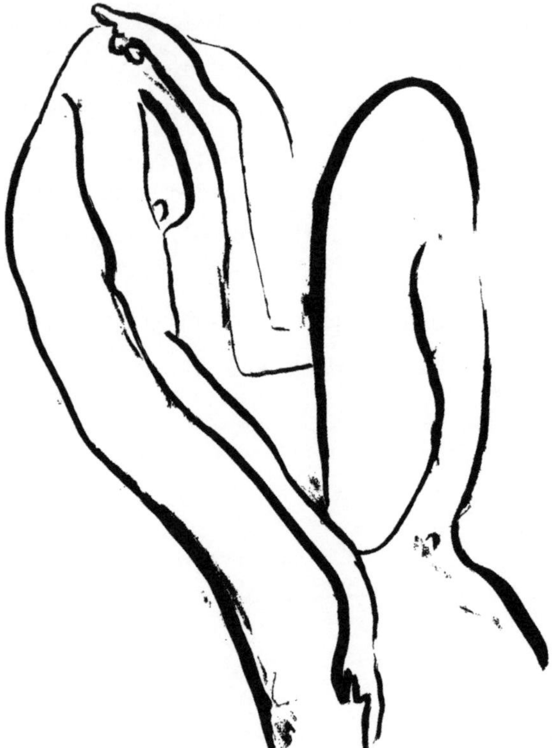

CAN'T BREATHE

Midnight, wake up, I can't breathe, my insides are
squeezing shut
My heart is racing, my chest is closing like my cords have
been cut

It feels like I'm choking from the inside, I can't speak or shout
It feels like there's a monster in me that's trying to pull itself out

I find myself replaying my life as agonizing seconds pass
And then, like a punch in the chest, I gasp and collapse

Panicking, panting, and I am so desperate for air
I am huffing and puffing awake in my own nightmare

Over and over and every night on repeat it seems
These little terrors are trying to kill me through my dreams

Begging for answers to my uncertainties into the blue sky
I make it to my twenty-seventh birthday, but it's an icy cold July

Afraid to sleep, my twilights are getting haunting
I'm waking up half-alive and it's getting daunting

Stuck in a desk job and I'm sitting miserably in my cubicle
Drawing up floor plans as I anxiously await tonight's missile

Living the American dream, the one that everyone seems to want
My unfulfilling accomplishments, my delusions tease and taunt

One doctor after another, none of you I can seem to trust
Yesterday it was asthma, but somehow today it's acid reflux
You're all overworked, rushed, you can't dedicate to my dis-ease
None of you talk to each other, can't find the missing piece

You're desensitized, you come by with your sandwich and a surprise
You give me three weeks to live with no sympathy in your small eyes

Deadlines at work and deadlines with my fading vitality
Playing with legos at my desk to fake all this normality

You say I need emergency surgery, but you don't seem so sure
Maybe it's something else, you say I can afford another week to explore

Now my liver is failing, oh wait, now it's sleep apnea
None of you can pinpoint the cause of my mysterious mania

Months after all the confusing whirlwind, you say it must be stress
My broken spirit wonders why you didn't think before to ask this

Carrying stress in my mind until my body becomes symptomatic
But you don't know how to ask the right questions and be holistic

No mention of therapy or learning why, you hand me anti-depressants
You would rather me numb my mind, you've given me no reassurance

It's much more rewarding for you to write me off with a paper for pills
Big pharmaceuticals in your wallets and I don't trust your chemicals

One pill to cure one thing, only followed by side effects
Another pill to cover those, it doesn't make any sense

Quiet and obedient, I have always given my voice away
Defeated and betrayed, now my body is making me pay

I'm breaking down and self-destructing from the inside
The monster in me is killing me and I can't figure out why

There must be more to my story, what could I be missing?
The causes of my stresses that I'm constantly dismissing

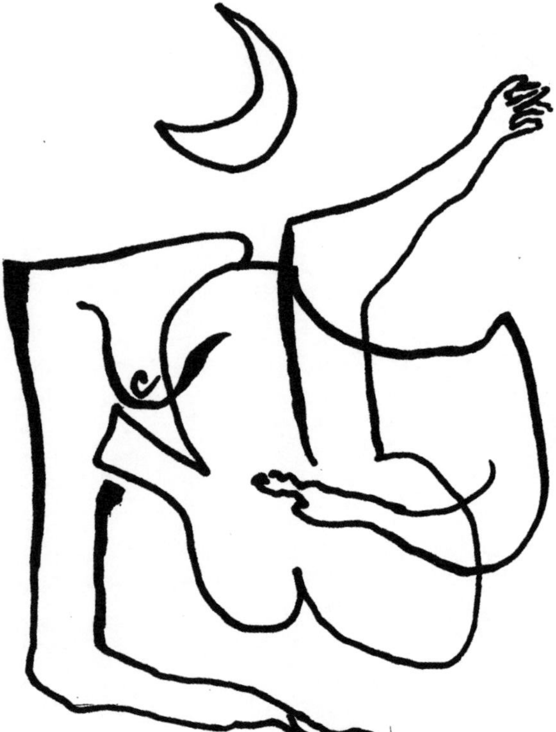

FISH ON THE MOON

Caught by a fishing line and pulled abruptly out of the ocean
I'm riding on a comet and colliding on the far side of the moon

Everything is upside down, I'm trying to swim in a navy mirror
I've burrowed myself into my very own Mare Imbrium crater

On the other side of the pyramid, no sun rays, no warmth
Flaming on the inside, suffocating, yet I'm cold to the touch

I wish for a different life, but I have everything I've been told to desire
Bury and burn my dismay from the disappointing reality in my internal fire

Monster in me urges me to redirect and go the other way
Violent urges in me to pull the plug and throw it all away

Pushing, pulling, guiding me by a cacophony of convincing ambition
Powering me, draining me, only fueling my inevitable depression

Voices bouncing through this dark lava and I feel so alone
Silencing the echoes, I'm losing sight of my comfort zone

Hardly skin and bones now, I can't even take a breath
Choking on my courage, I'm going to flip and flop to my death

Zero gravity hits as I flip and I'm falling up into space
How did I even get here? I'm not sure I know how to trace

Free-floating now, drifting further into the absorbing abyss
I'm holding on to nothing that's real, it's so treacherous

I'm made of degenerate matter like a white dwarf
Barely emitting light, I'm a forgotten stellar corpse

I'm either hardening into place or spiraling out like an asteroid
Somehow I've looped myself into this unpredictable
cosmic void

Searching for answers and I'm lost in the vastness
I can't see anything and I'm lost in the blindness

Scared, alone, nobody here to comfort me
Hey, Moon, what do you want me to see?

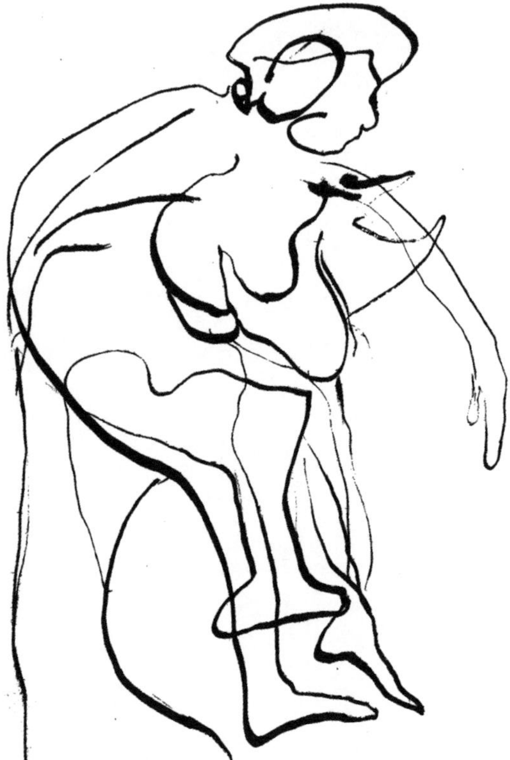

SUBLIMINAL GLITCH

A few years later now and I feel like I'm doing fine
New job, a faster pace, though I'm always out of time

My eyes are tired and my head is full of aches
Another work deadline, I'll do whatever it takes

Feeling the pressure of my life gets heavy, it's trapped me
Why does living feel so hard, why can't I just be happy?

Funny, I'm sitting here helping design lasting architecture
I can't even seem to hold up my own crumbling structure

Day after day these debilitating migraines get the best of me
Going through the motions, I'm a zoned-out brain-dead zombie

I used to be so put together, but now I'm just falling apart
I'm so irritated at myself, I need to snap the hell out of it

I'm sitting at my cold white desk and staring at my timed-out black screen
I feel so stuck, I'm a marionette puppet hanging from a million strings

I'm feeling the sting of loneliness, why does no one love me?
Why do I hate my life, why can't I ever let anyone near me?

The angry monster is still here and it's kicking me softly
Heart racing, mind spacing, and my eyes start to spin slowly

The room starts to whirl around and I can't see straight anymore
I'm losing my equilibrium, the monster is flicking my inner gyroscope

My arms start shaking and my body is convulsing
I'm losing control in the office, this is so embarrassing

Right in front of everyone like I'm the main headliner
Drawing unwanted attention like I'm a theatrical performer

Please don't look at me, don't watch me fall
I really don't want anyone to see me at all

I can't believe that I'm self-destructing all over again
I thought the monster inside me was dead and gone

Off to another specialist, here I go
More pills instead of solutions even though I say no

Brain scans and balance tests, my results are all clear
I don't want to die now, my thirtieth birthday is near

You say it's probably just stress, there seems to be no cure
You say it's all in my head, I'm totally fine, you seem so sure

You just patch me up and watch me walk away
Good enough for now, your job is done for the day

My body seems to be responding violently to all this stored tension
But my problems are not serious enough for you to find the connection

I don't even know how to begin this journey of searching
What is wrong with me, wouldn't it be obviously glaring?

Why do I choose to shut down and implode every July?
My sensitive body always seems to be triggered at this time

I need to slow down, need a break, need to coast
Maybe a simpler life is what I really need most

Maybe I'll try to meditate and see if I can get to the root of this
But these mindfulness apps sort of stay right on the surface

I know I have to dig deeper, is there another method?
A different way to access the things I keep embedded

Sleep meditation frequencies on Youtube, never heard of spiritual detox
417 Hz is supposed to release negative energy and remove my mental blocks

Maybe, just maybe, something will unblock
I'm sure there's plenty in my psyche to unlock

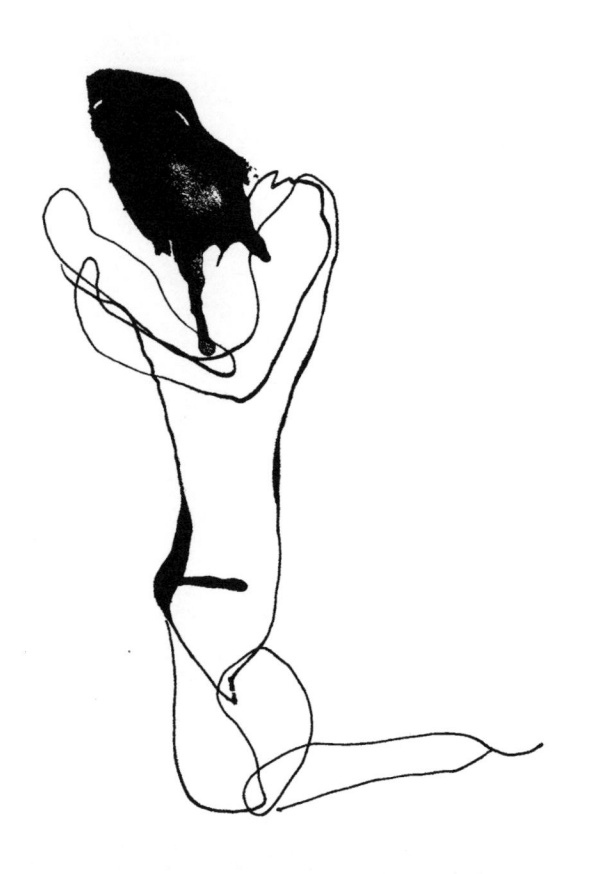

UNCOVERING THE TRAUMA

I wake up weeping from a terror much worse than my last
Stuck in a lost memory and replaying a story from my past

I thought I deleted this moment a long time ago
But I'm watching it live now like it's a Broadway show

You are the man I call Uncle, you have us all in your lair
Babysitting all the children, we are left alone in your care

The pizza just got here and I'm the last kid to wait in line
As my turn arrives you stop me and pull me to the side

You ask me if I can keep you company for a nice drive
Something is off, my gut is wrenching, and I feel it's a lie

Why just me? Please don't let me have to ride alone
I look around the kitchen, but no one else wants to go

I can feel my heart race and then slowly shatter
How come when I say no it doesn't matter?

I feel obligated to go, after all, you're like my uncle
I don't want to be rude, or worse, get into trouble

You want me to sit up front, you want me to be comfy
You ask me what music I like, but it feels so creepy

You start getting chatty, you want to know what I like
But then you place your right hand on my little left thigh

My internal alarm bells are blaring, oh, I wish I was wrong
I should have listened to my hunch, it was right all along

You touch my face and tell me my skin is soft, I freeze
Your hands make their way further down my body with ease
Your hands crawl all over me and you start grabbing my chest
I've hit puberty, breasts are growing, and you say you're impressed

You tell me I'm such a big girl now and that I'm so mature
You have been watching me all along and I don't feel so pure

I'm still just a kid, only a few weeks shy of turning thirteen
A cloudy July, why in the world is this happening to me?

You keep trying to go all the way and you're getting pretty close
My heart is about to explode and I just want to stay in my clothes

There's no way you would go all the way down there,
would you?
I'm freaking out, I can't let you touch that, what should I do?

I can't let you have me, I'll have to stop you on my own
But to act out against an adult, I have never been so bold

I whisper for you to stop and then slowly I get louder
I take your hands off my body and I couldn't be prouder

You think I am enjoying this and you seem dumbfounded
"Oh, you don't like it?" You want to finish what you started

I say I don't like it and you keep trying to convince me
I'm so scared, I feel so small, and I just want you off of me

You finally stop and drive back, swearing me to secrecy
You say my parents wouldn't like it and obviously, I agree
I'm supposed to be untouched and clean for my husband
Pivotal moment in my life, now I'm tarnished, cheapened

I am so ashamed for being too weak and too nice
I went against my intuition and I had to pay the price

Knowingly walked right into your not so sneaky laid trap
I'm more mad at myself for getting caught in your crap

Today I wake up sobbing and my eyes are hollow
Transported into the present and I still carry my sorrow

Tainted, horrified, stained, guilty, I feel so dirty
Another sleepless July, right before I turn thirty

I just cracked myself wide open, seventeen years of stress
Buried and anchored deep inside me and within my chest

Blacked out childhood memories playing back and forth
A mocking recollection of my evidently stunted growth

Past and present, I'm glitching between timelines
How could I have missed all the obvious signs?

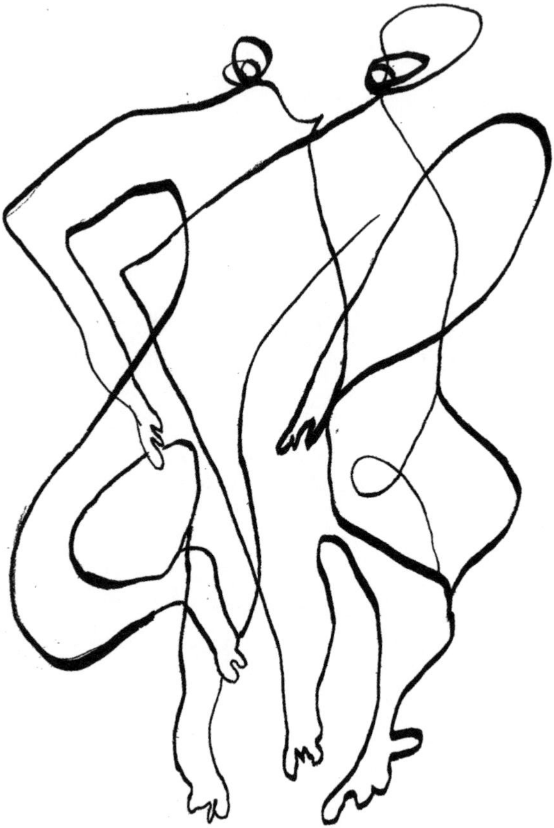

YEAR THIRTEEN

I can't believe you slaughtered my soul the other night
I'm too scared to say anything, I don't know what's right

I feel really guilty that I got myself into this shameful mess
If my parents find out, will they just be embarrassed?

I know it would hurt them to know that I got hurt
I don't want to hurt them, even if I am the one who is hurt

Thirteen years old and I will never learn how to be a girl
I will live on like a mannequin and shield my little pearl

Every night before bed I beat my blooming bosom out of agony
I plead, please stop growing, can't you see you embarrass me?

Every other weekend we go and visit you and your family
I throw a fit each time and never explain to my parents why

Numbing myself on the drive over, hardening my heart
Slowly stacking the limestones around me, this is the start

You're my dad's best friend and the moms and kids all get along
I can't be the one who pauses everyone's happy summertime song

Smiling at me from afar, I have to go say hi, your hands linger
Oh, you're testing my strength and putting me through the wringer

Weekend after weekend, I hold it all in, I grin and bear it
Stomach full of aches, of fear, and I'm always constipated
I'm filled with dread and I start mentally burying myself away
Turning survival mode on and I keep pretending that I'm okay

Only for so long though, yes, it all unravels a year after
One year of terror, of a brave face I have had to plaster

Your children sing praises of you and I can't take it anymore
I'm so angry, I can't help but spill our secret to your daughter

I beg her not to say anything, please no one can know
But she tells her mother anyway and downhill we go

The phone rings and someone wants to talk to me, it's your wife
She wants to know the truth, my worst nightmare is coming to life

Unexpectedly, you both show up at my house and force
me to speak
It's like a courtroom in my living room, my own home feels
tragic

You swear on the holy book and so do I
You have the audacity to say I would lie

I'm screaming at you now and everyone is watching the
shitshow
Sobbing in the center of the room, and I just want to be alone

Over and over going over all the details and the timeline
Fighting to prove myself, I am just reliving your crime
I don't want all this attention on me, I don't want to be seen
I don't want you to smile at me, you won't win, you're unclean

I run upstairs, lock myself in the bathroom, and turn the
exhaust fan on
Sink on full blast, the noises soothe me, and in my tears I drown

Your wife and my parents believe me, and thankfully so
We cut off all contact, and that's about as far as we go

None of us know what the next right thing to do is
Immigrant families caught in between two worlds

We will all live in shame now, this is who we will become
Painting smiles with strength on our faces, it's not a problem

I just have to move on now, no one else needs to know
Lost and confused, I have to get through this on my own

I just brush it under the rug and hope it will go away
I should keep it a secret, what will other people say?

No social media, resources, books, or therapy for me
It doesn't occur to me to ever look, let alone dare to see

I've been in a new school and I don't have other friends
I stay alone in my sorrows, there's no other way this ends

So, I close my eyes and imagine running away to another place
Dancing in the meadows wearing a flowy dress made of lace
No one else is here, just me, the sky, and all of the yellow buttercups
I wish I could stay here forever, I don't want to be around any grownups

The sun sets in another traumatic July, right before I turn fourteen
The sun sets on my happy days, if only I could wipe the slate clean

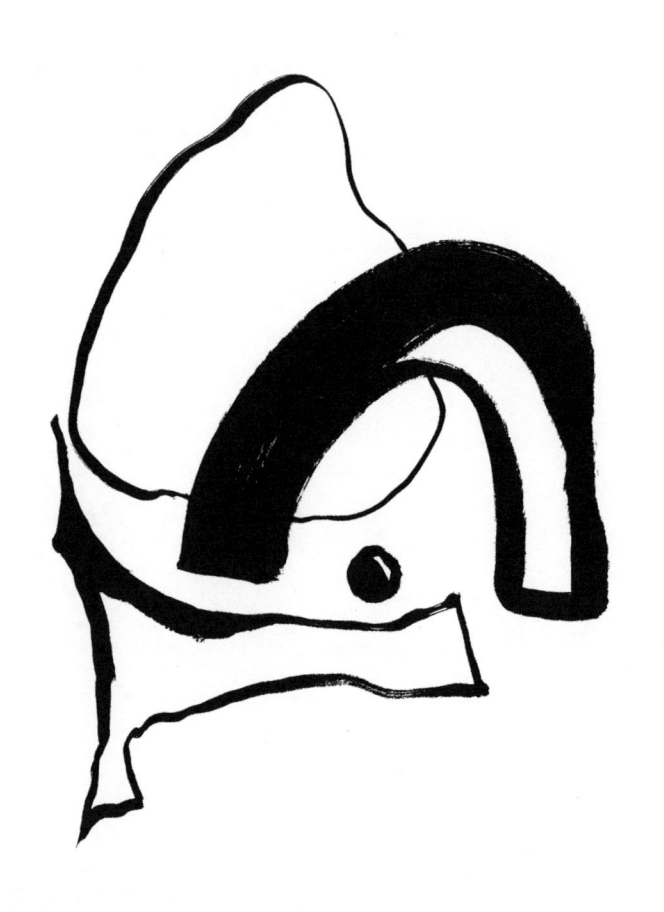

BUILDING MY PYRAMID

Wake up and get ready, it's really just another normal day
I'm learning to live in silence, it's much more simple this way

I am twelve, thirteen, fourteen, the years in this mess pass
New school each time and I'm always the new kid in class

I am a jaguar, a panther, a cougar, I am all the damn cats
Most importantly, I am a chameleon, I wear all the hats

Making my way through each sea of new desks
Always sitting in the back and closest to the exit

Trying to disappear, a little brown girl, and you always see me
Headbanging to heavy rock, these songwriters are just as lonely

9/11 has happened and I guess that it's true
It's hard to belong when I don't look like you

2000s America and suddenly I've become an overnight enemy
Terrorist nicknames and the cruel kids love to make fun of me

Ignorant kids hate me now and make jokes about Jihad
Ironic, after what Uncle did, I don't even believe in God

I'm supposed to follow the rules and stay scared
Fear of God and hell, I should be obedient instead

I'm supposed to keep my skin covered up, I'm confusing modesty with shame
But why does that matter? I was touched with my clothes on, I'm even more ashamed
The value of my body is dictated by religion, by culture, by everyone else but me
My value is reduced, it was never my choice, and I don't know what to believe

New school again, new mates, a new chance to start over
Discovering to be agreeable, my journey begins as a pleaser

Sixteen, I hate the color of my skin and my long hair too
The potential of a goddess, but I feel like a wannabe fool

Trying to blend in the crowds, but my brown skin is too different
Skin lightening creams, highlights in my curly hair now straightened

Overthinking my looks, I never know how to dress
Too pretty or not pretty enough, I am such a mess

I'm listening to hip hop, wearing thick red laces on my phat farms
Friends with everyone, yet no one knows me, I have all the charms

A black phantom with red lips, I love to hide in plain sight
I want you to see me, no, I don't, I can't seem to decide

Always listening, never talking, I am who you need me to be
I follow you and do everything you want, please don't leave me

Sensing what you need, I can peer right into your soul
I know what you need and I can make you comfortable

Outcasts taking me in, I'm way too nervous to talk to the cool kids
I'm a nerd, a loner, I'm your shadow who holds all your darkness

Insecurities deflecting, all my humor is self-deprecating
I see your awkward smiles, but I'm the only one laughing

I'm someone you used to know, someone you haven't met yet
I don't matter, I never did, I'm just a placeholder silhouette

Never staying in one place long enough to make my mark
I always flutter back to the fields in my mind like a meadowlark

Layers of pretty paint colors and I'm matching your wallpaper
Covering up how ugly I really am, it helps me feel a little prettier

I don't want the abuse to define me, except what if it does?
I'm still building my shell, looking for art, and gilding the doors

Intricately laying mosaic tiles, mirrors for you on my exterior facade
Hiding my true self behind them, I'm in the making of an innocent fraud

Don't you love to see yourself in me? I reflect all your pretty angles
Piecing together a torn lace dress, I am made of jagged-edged crystals

Deleting hints of feminine nature, associating softness with weakness
Don't need any boys, I'd rather be alone and grow my independence

I hate when the boys flirt, I don't trust when they're romantic
A reminder of my manipulating uncle, always an ulterior motive

I'm a protector, watching out for other girls, alert and sensing danger
I'm a projector, assuming the worst, and I won't let them get to her

Pushing down my twelve-year-old self, it's getting easier
It's like she never existed, I'm trying so hard to forget her

July after July, each a distant memory erasing from my aging frames
Dreadful birthday parties, forced smiles, my past burning up in flames

The sad song replays in my sleep until my heart is dull
Life goes on, y'all seem to move on, I'm lost in the shuffle

That night never happened, forget it, I'm almost there
I'm not that girl anymore, I can be someone who is better

Nowhere else to hide but at the very bottom of my mind
The sun goes down forever, the darkness leaves me blind

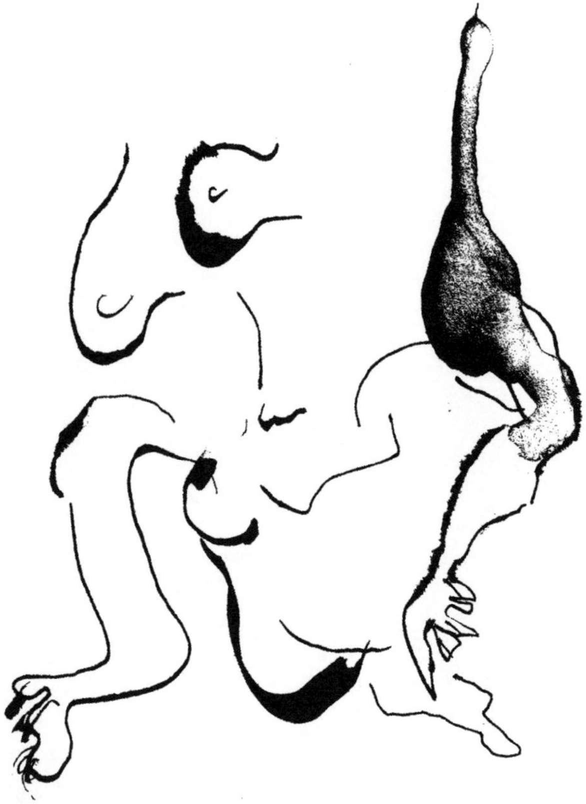

CAGED MEADOWLARK

Seventeen, eighteen, nineteen, teenage years fly by
Inside my dreams I run wild, but my outer self is shy

Scowl on my face, there's no smile, and I'm always angry
Too much damage in my eyes and it's easier to ignore me

I'm made of stone, love can never reach me through my polished finish
I'm that sad violin song, preserved underneath my gleaming oil varnish

Herded along with the crowds, the shepherd dogs wrangle me in
I want to escape into another world, but my options seem limited

Following the same dream that we are all handed in school
Just go to college, get the job, and begin life like a dumb fool

I don't want to be what the world keeps telling me to be
But I don't even know who else I am supposed to be

Feeling a tug from the inside, this is not the way I want to go
Only one path in my view and I decide to give others control

What's the point of destiny, why was I given this life?
Free will versus fate, do my choices affect my afterlife?

I reject old-school values and all the folklore, I don't want to be traditional
Twenty-one and living by my own ideals, I would rather be unconventional

Passing down customs, good and bad for generations
I discard them all because I can't tell the difference

Not cultured enough, not Asian enough, I rebel against it all
Losing even the best parts of me because I want nothing at all

I'm in training to be a good wife, I'm supposed to be domesticated
I don't want to be tamed though, married life seems so overrated

I don't believe in love or marriage, there's no such thing
I'm too dark-skinned anyway, who would give me a ring?

Home or work, men destined to have me as their subservient
Fuck all this, being a toy again is not my future intent

Why has the woman always been so strictly conditioned?
Live for everyone else in silence, so proudly suppressed

I don't want to be a wife, a prize, just an objectification
My life plans are already laid out for me, this is my obligation

Born into a world that hates me, I'll never be good enough
Purpose already decided, a predetermined fated handcuff

I need to be submissive, maybe a housewife, definitely a mother
I need to be independent, maybe a capitalist, definitely a leader

Outside world is different from my home, cultures clash
Stuck on track, standing in the center of a damn car crash
Inside I question and wonder, my internal compass spins haywire
I'm a lone wolf craving a pack, but I stay to the back of this empire

Crushing under the pressure of making the perfect impression
My existence only of representation igniting a perfect combustion

College is over and it's time to live my life my own way
But I'm not even sure what that means and I feel astray

I can't seem to understand or have sympathy for the restrained matriarch
Twenty-four, newfound freedom, but I'm still feeling like a caged meadowlark

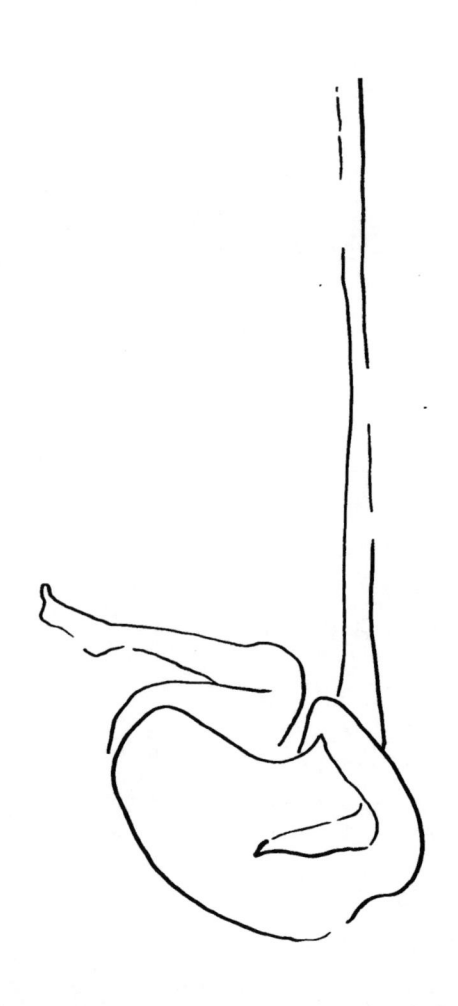

HANGED DOLL

Twenty-five, no direction, I keep going the way this old map routes
Something nudges inside me, I hesitate, I ignore it, I'm filled with doubts

Living on my own now and I'm already making a mess
All this new freedom has me making so many mistakes

I'm rebelling and pretending I never want to get married
Inside, I'm desperately craving for any guy to choose me

No dating allowed until marriage, all I can do is lie
My parents have no idea who I am, but neither do I

Harsh and afraid, I never meet you men with kindness
Or I'm bending over backwards like I'm utterly spineless

My dark brown skin isn't good enough for you, my culture hates it too
I stay under the sun, he loves me more than you do, so fuck all of you

Honestly, I would rather keep myself a little ugly
I don't actually want you to notice me or dare touch me

I only pick the players that I know have no desire to stay
All the wrong choices, but I keep the hope alive anyway

I've been fooling you all, letting you think I'm good enough
But I'm not even close, I hope you won't catch me in my bluff

Twenty-seven, my heart is desperate for loving validation
I overly nurture and get taken advantage of again and again

I'm just another oblivious girl for the ever curious devil
He has me in chains and I stay like a little hanged doll

I still won't speak my truth, I have no voice
I still act like a dummy, I have no choice

I'm trying to find my footing to get out of this noose
A black lace choker on my neck that I can't get loose

Centrifugal force of the earth holding me in place
Gravity of these torments and yet I feel weightless

Twenty-nine, single and alone, and I'm still not married
A disappointment to my culture, to myself, I'm devalued

My delusions are more pleasant where that other version of me lives
I want to join her and we could run free from it all like we're fugitives

So, I stay lost in the galactic meadows of my daydreams
The only place that keeps me from bursting at the seams

Everyone's playing in the summer breeze, but I fucking hate the end of July
I hate celebrating my birthday so much and I can't even remember why

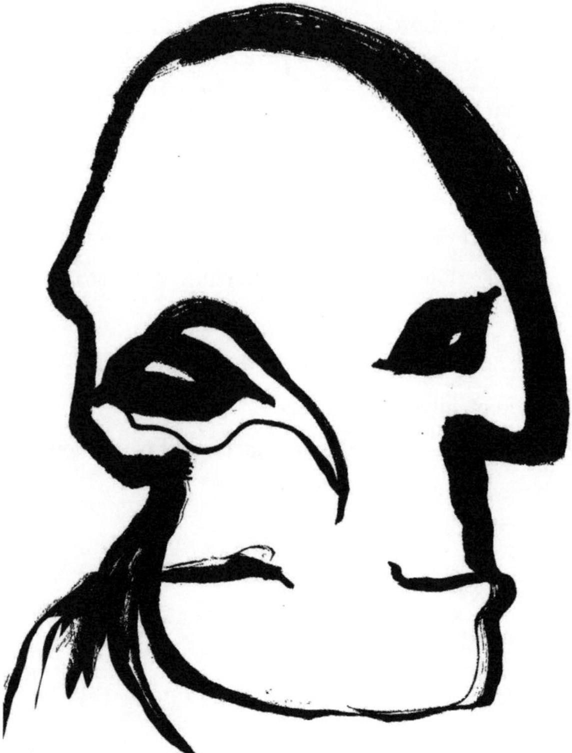

SATURN RETURN

Thirty years old, how did I not see, has it not been clear?
I'm still afraid of men and I am completely filled with fear

Is this my wake-up call, is this where I've been stuck?
I'm still twelve years old, this would be my damn luck

Oh, I learn Saturn has returned to greet me with this karmic lesson
Charted in my lucky stars, I'm destined for this timely depression

Icicles forming in my mind and I have fallen into a hole so deep
Nightmares storming in my waking life not just in my damn sleep

Friday night and I'm wailing into the forlorn winter skies
I'm all alone with no one to care about my heartbroken cries

The Wolf Moon listens, she understands my lonely grief
Just looking and talking to her brings me momentary relief

Hey friends, you care, yes, I know you do
But I feel like a burden, I can't tell you too

Would you notice if I was gone, would you even understand?
The empty smile on my face, do you notice that I pretend?

I tell you I'm doing great and we laugh, I feel like I'm trying
There's an ache in my stomach that reminds me I'm lying

Would it even matter if I died? I'm just another cog in the machine
Still a placeholder silhouette, an insignificant pawn in the grand scheme

Honestly, I'm not looking for your advice or even your pity
I doubt you can help me anyway, I've become so shitty

How did I get so completely out of whack?
Walking around with ten swords in my little back

Digging with my shovel, searching for meaning, I'm barely surviving
Craving for more, I feel nothing at all, my soul might need reviving

From all the reactions to becoming reactionless
I have no grip on myself, I am all over the place

I keep going from one extreme to the other
Losing my balance on both ends of the tether

I'm probably numbing myself on purpose
It seems much easier than feeling all of this

A mirror reflecting all your colors in the depth, I am so heavy
Sinking, drowning with this weight that I can no longer carry

Other side of a mirror, you can't see, I am no one, I am empty
Hollow, barely floating on, I am insubstantial and adrift at sea

My tank runs empty, autonomously on repeat, a slow perpetual motion
My head gets weary, subconsciously an echo, my monster is my captain

So, I'll sit at my desk, it's a perfect distraction
Focus on my job, a pointless plan of action

Dip up and down and wait for the next blow, I'm in a daze
Fall below, come back to zero, that's better than most days

All this time I never asked for help, shit, maybe I need therapy
Acting like it never happened, I thought I erased it from my memory

I told myself it wasn't that bad, it could have been much worse
I diminished my trauma and gave myself an exponential curse

First time to even search the term "sexual abuse" online
Fingers shaking, nerve wracking, I never thought to define

I don't even want to type the letters on my keyboard
It makes it way too real, I can't stand to look at the word

The monster inside me is sucking what's left of my energy
Eating me alive, I'm in defense mode, I'm tense and angry

Of course it's real, it's clearly bringing me to my demise
All I wish is to make it to another ultraviolet sunrise

All my old wounds brought back to the light
If I could just forget them and sleep tonight

Can't I just go back to the good old days
Where ignorance is bliss and happiness stays?

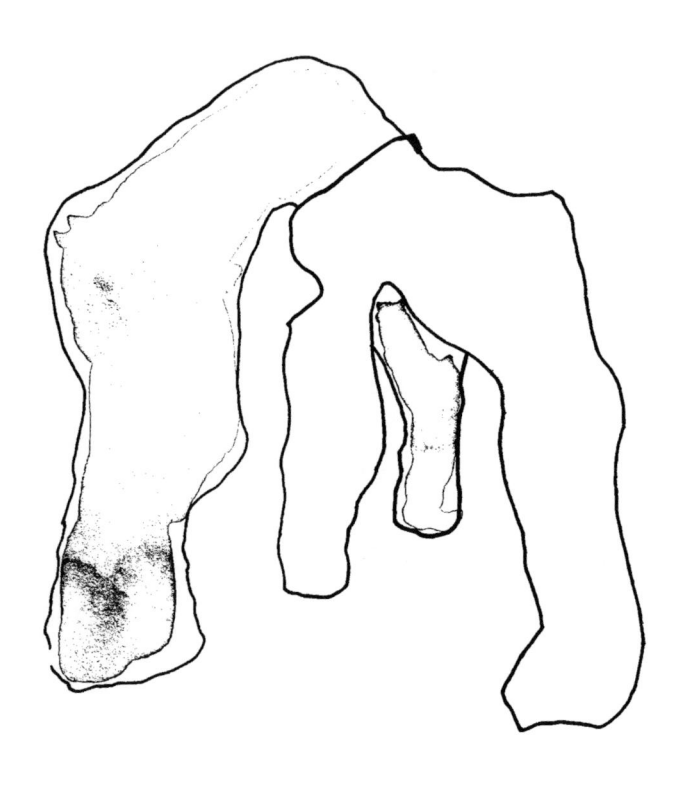

CAUGHT IN THE SEAWEEDS

I close my eyes and beg for a night of peaceful sleep
Instead my subconscious takes me to where my monsters keep

I open my eyes, but I can't see that girl in the meadows anymore
She seems to have left me for somewhere else to explore

I find myself caught in the seaweeds at the bottom of the ocean
I find myself caught in the maze of my own mind, I'm so damn broken

I can see the surface, there is a glimpse of distant sunlight
Dim and far away, like the fluttering ray of a child's flashlight

I feel like I'm a parody, the sun is shining on my misery
It makes more sense to just drown in this dreadful sea

I keep reaching for the stars, I want to get out of the dark
Sinking like bait through my bedrocks, I'm praying there's no shark

Frozen in place, winter in my mind, terrors slowly unfold
Listening for any secrets of the sea, but they are still untold

My legs are wrapped and the seaweeds tighten their grip
They won't let me go, they won't loosen or let me slip

My vision is colorless and I see nothing but gray
I think I need to be here, the darkness wants me to stay

I feel so old at thirty and everything seems so pointless
I feel like I'm wasting my life away, how do I get out of this?

All my accomplishments don't seem to matter because I'm still single
My career, my house, I should feel proud of myself, I'm so capable

Why does all this matter if I can't share this life with anyone?
There's a deep ache in my heart that keeps yearning for someone

I was so scared of being abused again that I let myself harden into a statue
But there's no love running in my blood, I'm made of epoxy glue

How could I let society, culture, and family shape me so much?
I was always a rebel, yet I was still formed and molded by
their touch

I have so much anger to unravel, who all can I blame?
I can point my fingers, but I am the one hanging onto shame

Forever condemned and living a lifetime of aloneness
What did I do to deserve this eternal emptiness?

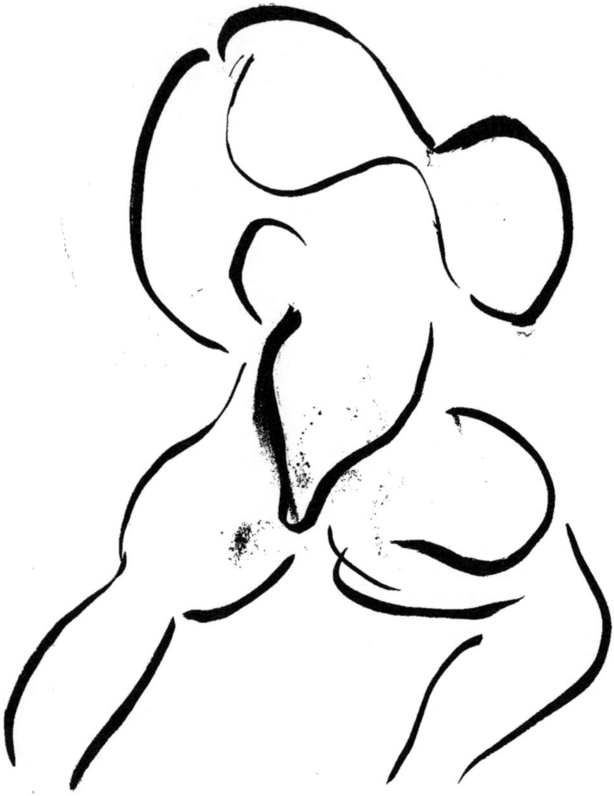

UNLOVABLE

Life goes on, leaves turn green, and I'm trying to hang on
Just get back to work with my pretend happy face on

The world is now caught in the midst of a pandemic
I'm alone at home and I have all this extra time to think

I don't mind the space to be alone with my thoughts
No distractions, no puppet strings calling all the shots

I'm lonely at home, but I can't really go out
It's lonelier with you, I so obviously stick out

Looking for me inside of you, but you are lost too
I can't even love myself, why the hell would you?

Your face is laughing, but it's mute to my ears
I can see you smiling, yet I can sense your fears

I can tell my presence is bringing you down
You miss my smile, you don't care for my frown

You probably hate me and yeah, I can tell
But there's no soul in me, I'm just a shell

I'm here, I promise, I just don't know what to do
I'm stuck inside this bronze statue staring back at you

I know I should say something, but instead, I just hold it
I am filled with shame, my stomach is always bloated

Bed, work, bed, I'm living the most bare minimum repeat
Days bleed together, my nights begin to fill with unspoken grief

Another night, another meltdown under the moon as she watches me cry
Stuck sitting at the bottom of the staircase, I'm too heavy to get up and try

What is this sadness telling me, why do I feel so lonely?
I don't deserve your love and I have never been worthy

You would not want me anyway, I'm carrying so much baggage
If only I could drop them, they're too much for me to manage

My calls aren't being answered, but I'll still say my prayers
I try to snap myself out of it and crawl all the way up the stairs

Sad thing is, you won't even hear what I'm saying
You say you love me, but I know you're just playing

All these songs of true love and heartbreak on the radio
But my heart broke before it ever had a chance to grow

The most painful Anemoia of a love never begun
A fairytale never written, a song never sung

Achingly longing for what could have been
A melancholy orchestra only playing in my dream

Everyone's settled in love and I think I'm missing out
Everyone's settled in fears and I think I'm lucking out

I'm tumbling up and down and I can't keep it together
Moments of laughter followed by sobbing right after

Let me push you away, I want to be alone in this emo song
I will come back to you one day, I just don't know how long

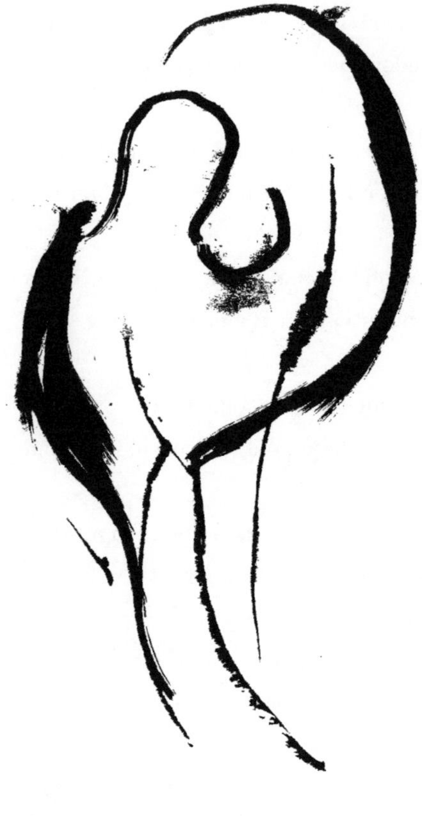

WITHERING AWAY

Spring is fading, winter in my mind, I'm a fucking ghost
There's a monster in me and I'm sure it hates me the most

Weekend escapes and it's fun in that moment
But I come back home and I feel the aloneness

Another month, another dip, unpredictable series of ups and downs
My roller coaster of shaky emotions seems to have no bounds

My farmhouse sink is full, my dirty dishes are stacking up
My laundry basket is full, my pretty clothes are piling up

I can't even recognize that girl in the mirror
I'm withering away, I don't even know her

Haven't left my bed in days, I can only get up to pee
Exhausted, can't sleep, can't move, I'm feeling so lazy

I am eating less, I have no hunger, no desire
I am losing weight, I have no strength, no fire

My pupils are shallow and filled with despair
My face is worn out, my big brown eyes are even puffier

My lips are dry and they flatline across my face
No more smile, there are minimal signs of life in its place

All this distress, my hair is falling out chunk by chunk
My luscious locks are shedding, I need to get out of this funk

My skin looks dull, and my periods are getting spotty
Not feeling like a human, it's like I've become robotic

So much for not feeling pretty, I can see my most ugly flaw
I'm watching my all of childhood truths eat through me raw

Spirit angry, mind empty, soul searching, it's all crushing
No way I am getting out of this alive, my body is breaking

I have no control over my body, outside I'm frozen, inside
I'm spiraling
I can't go on like this any longer, but I don't know how to
stop digging

Life was never sunshine and rainbows, but it was never so sad
How can my trauma from long ago still make me feel so bad?

Scrambling and scribbling in my notebook on my phone
I'm not worthy of love, I am too ugly, I am too broken

How much longer is this going to have a hold over my life?
What am I suffering so much for, why is a living hell my price?

I start writing away, documenting each physical downfall
Noting down my ugliest thoughts that come to life at nightfall

Auto-pilot on, I'm barely here, I would rather die
I'm walking dead and wondering if it's time to say goodbye

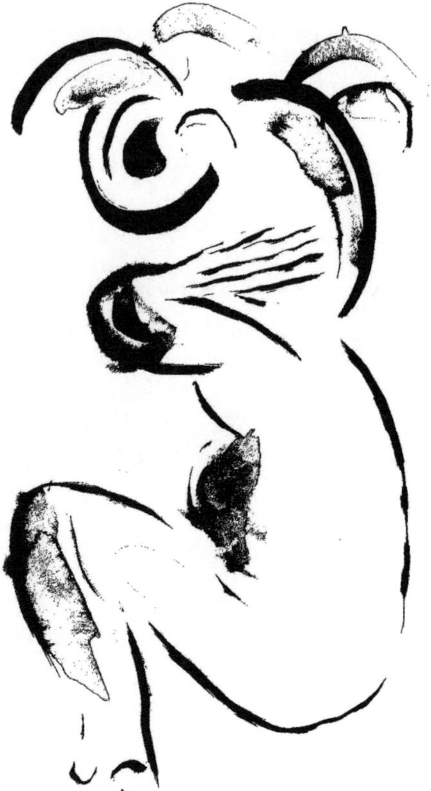

FIVE OF CUPS

I look at the sun and cry, but at least I can feel something
A bit alive, much better than being numb and feeling nothing

My thoughts are out of control, they won't stop racing
My mind is fueling my legs and I can't stop pacing

Sunlight's blazing my eyes now, it's way too bright
Slither back into the shadows, I belong in the night

I'm trying so hard to keep my sobbing to a minimum
It's not working and I keep falling into a dark oblivion

I've never let myself feel emotions like this before
My spirit is tearing me apart and exposing my core

No other way to explain how I'm feeling bummed out
My body's self-defense is keeping my mind numbed out

It hurts too much, I am running out of patience
It's too hard to live, I am running out of options

Days go by, I just try to keep moving, my fear concentrates
I try not to worry as the arrival of my death precipitates

That girl in the meadows feels far away, I can't reach her
Would she even be my friend, would she let me near her?

I've been digging in the past for answers, but I don't feel so brave
I peek out and see that all I've been doing is shoveling my own grave

I'm so deep in this black hole, barely alive, I'm comatose
I used to know how to cope, now I'm not even fucking close
Lying wide awake staring at the ceiling, I've become nocturnal
Lying comfortably with the devil, we're planning my funeral

I'm on the edge of existence, I'm not sure anyone would even care
Ruminating round and round while juggling five cups in the air

The evil in me is taking over and I'm feeling possessed
Can't think of anything else now, I'm becoming obsessed

Stop, just stop, why do I always take it this far?
Chill out, take a breath, and make a wish on a star

I have too much of this world to see, I have to be okay
Just close my swollen eyes and hope to make it to another day

I know I have to face the abuse, my past, and feeling unworthy
I have to release this from my mind and body, so I can be free

It's 4:44 and my angels remind me that a new tomorrow is coming
I wonder which colors the sun will shine through the clouds in the morning

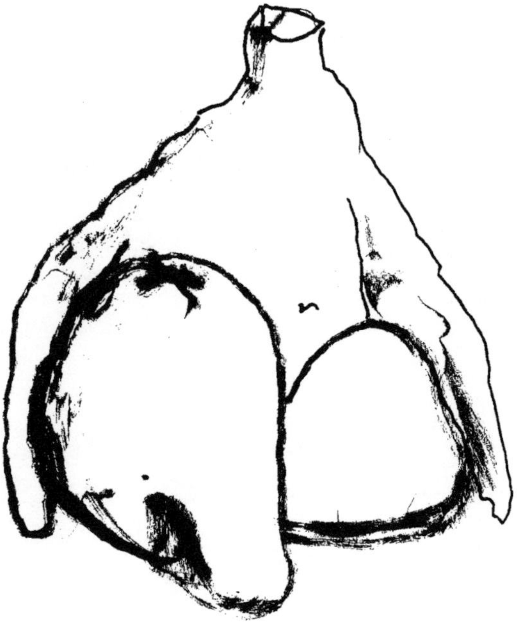

MOUNTAINS OF HOPE

I'm getting really desperate to not let myself drown
Maybe I just need to take myself out of this busy town

The mountains are calling and I haven't felt it like this before
It's a hot sunny summer and I'm sort of feeling frantic to go

Travel slowly opens back up, the pandemic still carrying on
I spontaneously buy a plane ticket and I'm going it alone

Touchdown, new place, the winds are already lifting me
Nothing more relieving than an abrupt change in scenery

I rent a cheap little car and start making my way into the unknown
Pushing the car to its limits, I'm doing all this on my own

Accelerating to the middle of nowhere and I can breathe again
Climbing higher and higher and my spirit begins to ascend

Suddenly, it's quiet and I can slow down time for a bit
Between the breeze and the lakes, this place is my respite

Trees instead of columns and hills instead of buildings
I can feel something inside of me starts tingling

Hiking along, I find a rushing stream and walk up to it
Big flat boulders along the side make for a perfect spot to sit

The sun is hot, but the water is not
I slip my feet in and try not to freak out

The freezing cold shocks me back to life, oh, the irony
I feel like the universe loves playing games with me
The smell of the earth is a comfortable nostalgia
Dirt on my brown skin and I'm blending in my camouflage

Soggy shoes drying in the hot sun as I hike back to the center
Refreshed now, I'm ready for my next random adventure

I climb into a ski lift and ride up as high as it can go
Bouncing along the cables, my feet swinging above the treetops below

Watching people look like ants as they meander to the top
I wonder what they think of me when they stop and look up

I jump off the lift and view the sights from my 13,000' elevation
Scanning like an eagle, I'm trying to keep up in an esoteric meditation

Mountains are a solid source of wisdom, of grounded magic
An undeniable case of something humble, yet majestic

Writing away, finally a few of my most beautiful thoughts
My not so broken moments captured in poetic snapshots

A reminder to look back on my moments of greatness
Green flags of hope when I'm in my moments of weakness

I wish I didn't feel so unworthy all the time, but right now I'm okay
I wish I could erase this pain forever, how did I get this way?

The monster in me is calm for now, I breathe deeply, in and out
Maybe it needs the fresh air, maybe I'm starting to wear it out

I flip back to my older scribbles, I cry as I read my words
A mental place of disgrace, now I actually have no words

Remembering how small I am in the grand scheme of things
Helps ease my mind and take the pressure off of my being

I feel alive again, even if it's just in this moment
Slowly finding my calm in the sierra, so potent

I want to be that girl of my wildflower dreams, I want to be better
I want to wander and explore, I have a whole world to chase after

Grounded and solid, I wonder how many before me have knelt
This is the closest to God or anything spiritual I have ever felt

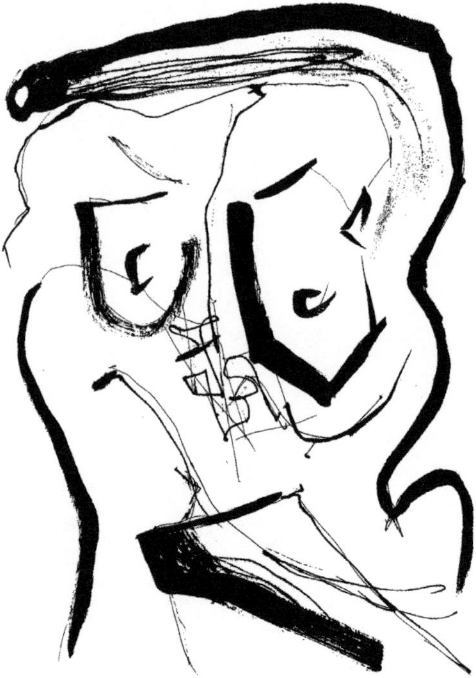

FINDING ENCHANTMENT

I met a massage therapist downstairs in the hotel lobby
She says she can do reiki too like it's her secret hobby

A kind of energy healing, I hope this can heal my core
I have no idea what this special session has in store

An hour passes by and she's tapping me awake
My chakras were blocked, she made them activate

I can actually feel the energy shifting within me
A burst of life stirring inside, I really hope this will fix me

There's a sweet crystal shop in the center of town
Feels like a candy store with so many gems for my crown

Magical little stones, tell me about your superpowers
I'm getting found in this place, I can spend all my hours

I don't know too much about this enigma just yet
But I'd love to keep a piece of this pretty earth in my pocket

Amethyst for intuition, rose quartz for love
Please sign me up for all of the above

I don't even know if all of this shit works
But I'm desperate enough to try all these quirks

I'll take all the fucking magic I can get
Anything to turn around this period of suffering I regret

Cleanse these rocks as they cleanse my soul
Slowly, but surely my heart is feeling full

Seven different chakras, energy points, and an aura
Balancing the rainbow, there's so much to explore
From the cosmos into my crown, to my third eye, and through my throat
My heart, solar plexus, sacral, and down to my root

I'm diving deeper into this spiritual rabbit hole
The universe is full of hidden secrets, it's so mystical

One last exploration, confidence radiating from my solar plexus
A two hour drive winding and curving into a mythical nexus

I make my way to a secluded oasis of therapeutic hot springs
To bathe for hours in the mineral waters for natural healing

Soaking in sodium and magnesium like I'm a warm spicy stew
Fermenting any anguish away in my own witch's boiling brew

Staring at the passing clouds and I begin to imagine
My soul is flying back into my body and I am human again

This trip to the mountains is just what I needed
So simple to be alive, finally I am beginning to feel it

I'm feeling one with the world and it's so comforting
The honor of basking in this marvel is beyond rewarding

Mountains, rivers, and solitary moments
I can feel a bit of peace and now crave my silence

I close my eyes and fill my chakras with the white light
I think I can actually reach the stars tonight

I gaze off into the midnight sky filled with mystery
A concoction of depth, wonder, and curiosity

Black holes pulling me in and swallowing me whole
Feeding off of my energy, but I don't feel so alone

Sitting with my sadness, I know I have to let myself grieve
The light needs the dark and I don't have to let them unweave

Grieving the happy kid I could have been in my stolen childhood
Grieving the broken version I became in my tormented young adulthood

Finding beauty in the gloom and the magic of pain
Depths of feeling, of making wild turns, driving me insane

I have nothing to be ashamed of, I never did anything wrong
I was an innocent child with too many burdens to carry on

I lost control of my own wheel, and created my own storm
Anger powered my winds in the night, my sails had torn

Releasing the shame from my soul, from my heart, from my skin
Enough is enough, wounds hurt the worst before healing begins

I can't differentiate between the night sky and the black sea
Horizon line blurs, mirrored starry skies, I make my own galaxy

I want to fly through the skies and get lost up there forever
I'd rather stay above, but I know it'll soon be over

You'd think I'm high
I swear I'm lit off my own mind

Everything feels new, but it was here all along
A sigh of relief as I have my golden lenses on

I can feel my spirit finally awakening
Hey, Monster, is this what you have been wanting?

I can't believe it's another summer, another July
It's different this time, I'm coming back to life

I really didn't think I'd make it to thirty-one
Maybe, just maybe, this time I have won

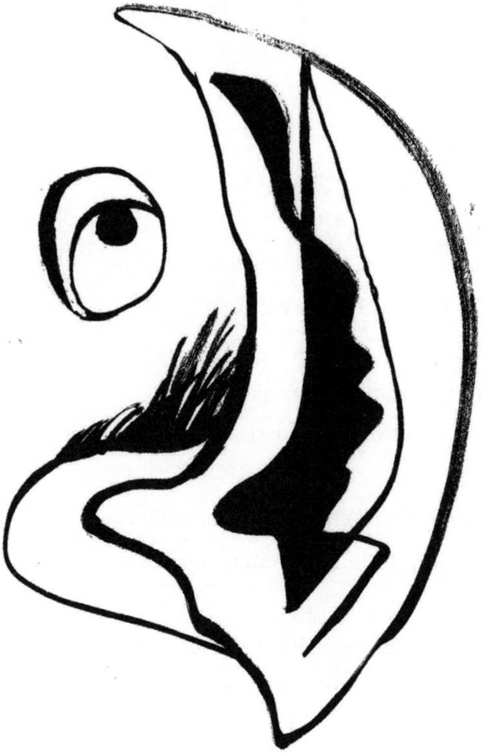

LUMINESCENT GLOW

The moon is void of course, she's swimming in the emptiness
I close my eyes and start slumbering into the haziness

I'm standing at the edge of a cliff encircled by water
Turbulent waves splash on the rocks and it's so much darker

The clouds hang low, I look around and all I see is foggy peril
I'm on the deep end staring right into the red eyes of the devil

Winds are heavy and almost pushing me off this tower
It's scary as hell to jump, but maybe that is part of my power

Lightning strikes, nothing to lose, my fear fades as I leap
Ice cold water hits my skin, I dive all the way down deep

I open my eyes underwater and see a distant luminescent glow
Way beyond the surface, I'm sifting through what's below

It's thick and murky, but this time I'm not as scared
I follow the glow, going further than I've ever dared

Floating around in the middle of the dark black sea
Golden orbs flashing with snapshots of my memory

It's warmer as I swim closer to where the light radiates
It's like an embrace full of grace as the truth emanates

Happy moments of my life crystallized into place
It's all right here, the brilliant captures of my face

Photographs of my big laughs, my past and future is all here
Peering into my Akashic records, a timeline in my mind, it's so clear

I can see myself smiling and I can still feel the buzz
My whole life is in this dying sea of what once was

I keep choosing to remember the scowls, but there were smiles too
I see promises of new things to be happy and sad for, yet to be true

Reroutes, new paths, new future endings are being luminesced
New hopes in my eyes, I can choose to manifest what
comes next

My true self is alive and well as far as I can see
I have the strength to create who I want to be

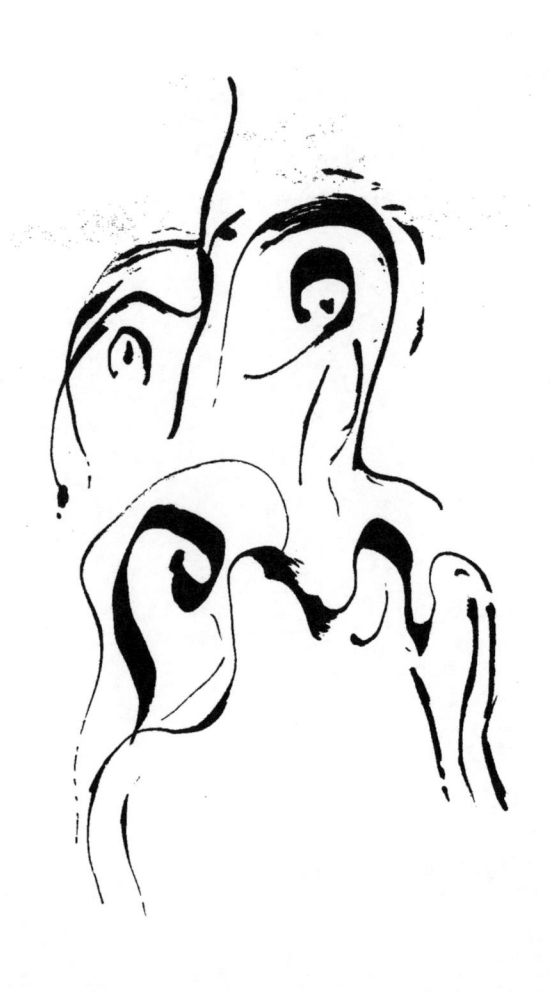

LITTLE LION STRENGTH

Day by day I'm planting new habits and making new choices
Little by little I'm getting better at quieting my obsessive
inner voices

Back to basics, wake up, drink water, go for a walk, watch
the sun
I don't need anyone's permission to shine, I can turn my
own light back on

I am feeling much more alive and better than ever
I think I am finally beating this game of solitaire

I know I'm alone, but I don't really feel lonely
Either way, I really would love some furry company

I bring home a kitten, I can make my own little family
An unusual gray tuxedo with a soft pink nose, I call him Billy

So regal and commanding, a true tiny king
Fierce and full of life, a brand new beginning

His warm presence fills up our entire home
So much love, I never would have known

He follows me everywhere and we feel so connected
We stay wild and free in our modest palace of pretend

My little lion tamer except I have been the raging beast
Independent, yet devoted, he teaches me inner peace

He loves himself without any shame, he is my heaven-sent teacher
I have so much to learn from this wise innocent creature

His loyal companionship gives me courage and hope
A symbiotic relationship of love and I know I can cope

He makes me feel so child-like and innocent again
A little giddy and silly before reality begins to set in

I finally feel like I'm pulled back up to a more appropriate composure
Sensing that I'm balanced for now, but I still want some kind of closure

Releasing my pride, I know that I need a helping hand
I can't do let myself drown again, I can't let myself go mad

I have a sweet kitty now and I want to be the best mommy for him
I need to be free of all my tortured misfortunes and find my lasting rhythm

I'm making so much progress, but the pain is still there
I'm ready to talk to someone, I'm finally ready to share

Conducting so much research, scouring all the therapists
Not many in the city that are child sex abuse specialists

I wish I could find a brown girl, someone who can relate to me
But she doesn't seem to exist, I'm not sure if someone else would get me

I finally find someone that I'm hopeful will be suitable
Hesitant, I make an appointment, this is half the battle

Apprehension sets in as I drive myself to my initial visit
My heart begins to race as I walk up to the clinic

It's my first time in therapy and I'm no longer feeling as weak
I've been cleansing my throat chakra and I can finally speak

The secrets pour out of me and I can't help but cry
This leech has been feeding off me and bleeding me dry

It is such a release and I know this is a long quest
But I feel so good just to get this off of my chest

I have a long road ahead
But at least I'm not dead

QUEEN OF PENTACLES

Early morning sunshine beaming through my bedroom window
Watching nighttime fade into an ombre painting of blue
and yellow

Billy snuggles next to me, his warm body soothes my heart
We are becoming each others' safe haven of comfort

Feeling creative these days, I've been growing my own garden
I may be planting these seeds, but they are my oxygen

I buy a feeder and fill it up with a gourmet of wild bird seeds
I can't wait to see what kind of new friends it brings

I throw my banana peels and kitchen scraps in the soil
Nourishing my land, keeping it lush and fertile

I don't mind being dirty, in fact I think I love it
Muddy hands, walking on the mossy pavers barefoot

The earth is touching my skin and it's like I'm back in the mountains
Familiar petrichor in the atmosphere, but I'm just at home in my garden

Learning how to slow down, be human, accept my flaws
Stronger boundaries, saying no, putting my grief on pause

The puffy white clouds move along and the darker gray ones roll in
I don't want to stop playing outside now, I'm having way too much fun

The cold rain drops start pouring down and it feels like a renewal
Cleansing the grounds, my face, and my energy, it's a healing revival

I run inside and place my pots outside so they can load up
Collecting all the rainwater, I let the abundance fill my cup

I'm running around, looking up, and soaking it all in
I can't help but laugh at myself as I play in the rain

The rain drops settling on my skin, I feel alive, I'm alive
Worthy or not, the rain still waters me and keeps me alive

Gardenias, jasmine, and majesty palm trees
Squirrels, bluejays, butterflies, and bees

So many fresh flowers blooming throughout
Thriving and full of life, where once there was drought

A cardinal comes by and he's the happiest tint of poppy
Like the midnight sun burning in July, I name him Ruby

A bunch of other birds fly in to visit me everyday
Dropping seeds everywhere while they eat and play

Fallen seeds blossom into my favorite cheery sunflowers
They plant them for me as I'm channeling my inner Venus

They're singing songs for Billy and I and we listen to them with delight
They whistle poems about love and breath, they give us both insight

Well to me anyway, Billy is trying to hunt them from the window
There's so much excitement going on like I have my own show

Can't wait to finish work so I can play in my garden these days
Slowly releasing the pain and clearing up this ancient haze

I'm starting to feel more comfortable in my own skin
I'm learning to love who I might have always been

I feel so good now, but I know the worst is not over at all
I turn my face to the moon at noon until it's time to fall

From feeling so lonely to enjoying my solitude
I never knew how much I could adjust my own mood

Shedding layers, I'm staring at myself, shattering my mosaic tiles
Painting my skin brown with the dirt, letting my crazy curls go wild

Walking and mental processing under the oak tree canopies
Saving me from dwelling in looping outdated memories

Eating fresh veggies, cooking more, and drinking more water
Cleaning my house and my habits, one room after the other

I guess mother nature is my new promising persuasion
Casting spells with my antique wand like I'm a magician

An irrefutable existence of life, I see there is no limit
Through me, because of me, and even with me in it

The sun sets in my patio, rays of golden shine onto my Eden
Every night is a new color picture show, revealing what's hidden

This pretty movie is what's keeping me alive at this point
Finding some kind of connection to what seems so distant

I am so happy on my own, I'm flourishing in my own energy
I can't stand the thought of mixing back in with society

The pandemic gave me a chance to explore my feminine delights
Work from home, from bed, an escape from the bright lights

I have to protect everything I have just created
But it's a matter of time that I need to reintegrate

I know I can't stay in my safety net forever
I'm just so afraid of breaking everything I've put together

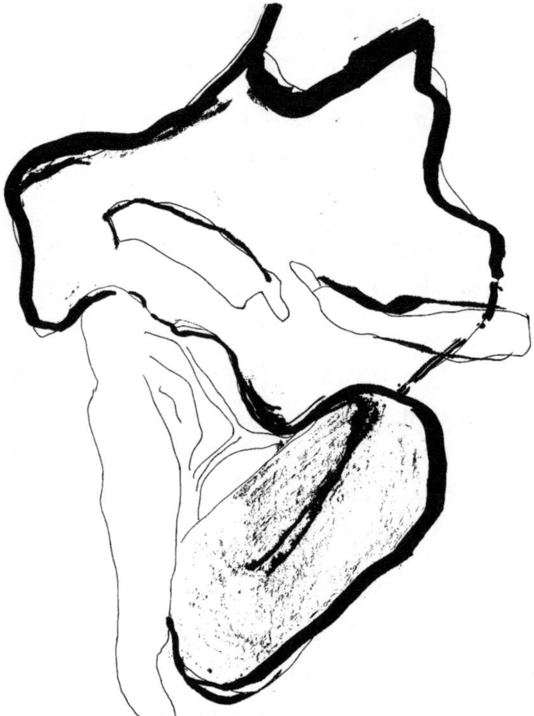

SILVER CEREMONY

Slowly return to the office, it's time to leave my safehouse
Nice to see you all again, but I can feel the creeping chaos

The strength of my fortress walls can't protect me out here
All the noise and fog are forcing their way into my sphere

Old hectic routines just like before the pandemic
How on earth did we learn nothing from that panic?

Back to gossip, chit-chat, and filled-up calendars
Low vibrations engulf me and I'm caged with fellow prisoners

You're all pulling me in so many different directions
I say yes to everything, I'm feeling all the overstimulation

Promotions and bonuses and endlessly climbing this ladder
Dangling pyrite prizes in the sky that I'm dying to chase after

Propaganda on billboards, constant reminders in my vision
No off button on this auto-pilot, absently riding into oblivion

Watching myself being manipulated in third person
A robot getting close to the bounds of this fucking simulation

I'm thrown off my balance, I can feel all my old anxiety
I'm trying not to conform back into this illusion of reality

I can feel the dormant anger brewing within
That little monster in me wants attention again

Like the flip of a switch and I'm falling right back down
I'm struggling to keep my peace with all of you around
I'm surrounded by blatant avoidance and cheap addictions
Trying to feel anything other than the truth, drowning in conflictions

What are the odds that I felt happier at home alone?
This change in pace has me designing my own gravestone

Haven't I been healing, how much rage do I have left?
I've been ignoring this part of my life and it feels like a theft

I really thought I was doing better, but I'm ready to blow
I hate being around you all now and I'm letting it show

I'm absorbing your emotions, the thin line blurs
Anxious and heavy, is this pain mine, or is this pain yours?

I can see you all repeating your hell loops over and over
I'm standing in the eye of the storm holding a four-leaf clover

All my feelings of shame and guilt are back
My body hates me again, and I'm under attack

You rip me open and shine a light on my shadows
Anger, insecurity, bitterness, and what's left of my sorrows

I'm a fireball burning everyone in my wake until they drown
Riding on undulating waves that always crash us back down

I used to be so good at hiding my tormented misery
Now I'm on display like a Picasso blue period piece at the gallery

Acting out in public as I'm caught in between two realms
Waking up on stage as I'm trying to take back control of the helm

Cry on my way to work, and on my lunch, I cry some more
Cry in my closet and let myself fall asleep on the floor

I don't think I can be who you want me to be
But I don't know how to escape this and be the real me

You may be a vain vampire, but I let you vacuum my energy
When am I going to learn to spend my pentacles wisely?

Tired of being numb and tired of being explosive
Tired of rusting away and tired of being corrosive

I look at Billy and tell him I can't be his mommy anymore
Tears in my eyes, I don't want to live this life anymore

I spy with my pretty little eye that turquoise chef's knife
You gave it to me last July, now I want to use it to slice my life

The metal blade shines my red devil eyes right back at me
I'm wearing sanguine lenses, no wonder my view is angry

The things I hate so much about you
Are just the things I hate about me too

I thought I was kind, but have I been a monster all along?
Suddenly, I feel so exposed, am I too far gone?

I've been so quick to judge, it's so easy to project
But it's my own ugliness that my armor is trying to protect

No, no, I know better now, it's not you, it really is me
You are the mirror of my wounds I have not been able to see

There is something in me that tells me to keep going
All these ups and downs have got to mean something

I'm still stuck on the wrong path, on the wrong side of the track
I'm still living the predetermined life that I can't seem to hack

I can see my own hell loop now and I pray it will soon end
I just want to live in a sunny paradise state of mind again

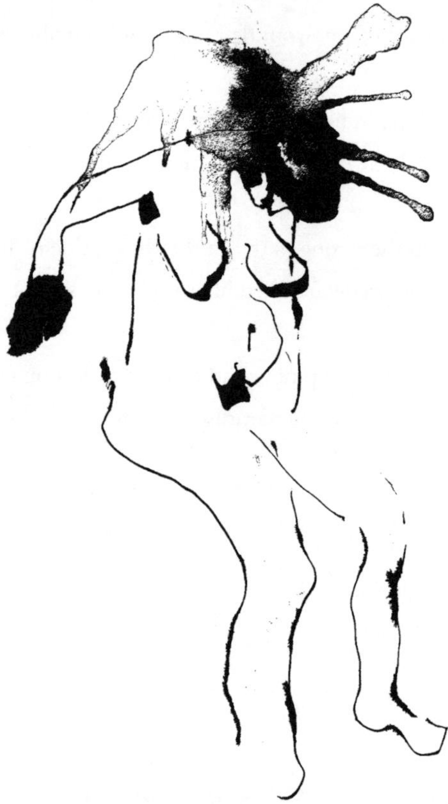

SKELETONS IN THE TRENCHES

Closing my eyes and returning to my wildly vivid dreams
I wake right back up in the midst of the ghostlore winter seas

Glancing into the void beyond, what else is here for me to see?
I'm just following my instincts this time with no moonlight
to guide me

The new moon is a seed of hope planted in the darkness
The shadow always remains, a reminder of equal balance

The grounds are in pain and they are crying out for relief
Tossed plastics, broken glass, and I'm staring in disbelief

I'm used to the dark now, an ambience I have almost b
egun to adore
Slipping on rocky sandstone as I trek along the sediment
seafloor

There's a wreckage ahead, sunken solar barques faded into
shades of fawn
Searching for Ra, I'm venturing in and out of smoky quartz
crystal ships at dawn

Navigating my way through all these sepia reminiscence
Particles of dust made of dead plants and marine animal remnants

The deeper I go, the lower vibrations I let myself feel
Shining my light and exposing what remains to heal

An overwhelming feeling of pain much greater than mine
Poverty, depression, hunger, it doesn't feel lovingly divine

Further along I think I can see a fish drifting closer
Except it's a swimming skeleton with a face of pure horror

It brushes against me and crawls into my foot
Wincing in pain, I can feel it swirling in my blood

I'm smashing its carcass and tearing off my own skin
Pulling out the spiky bones as fast as I can

Colonialism, corruption, we're all just animals in this circus
Why are we not all worth the same? A crumbling injustice

The bones get bigger in my hands as I yank them out
I'm scrambling and going crazy and I wish I could shout

Borders and walls to keep us sheltered, yet we stay fearful
Incurious, we choose to live in our ignorant safety bubble

I see a shadowy mist of more bony fish flying towards me
A haunting faint glow like ghastly candlelight in the sea

Judged for wanting anything different than the right way implied
The west way isn't the only way, I'm living in the hollow divide

My feet sink in the dense sands and I can't shake free
Terrified, I'm anchored somewhere I don't want to be

I wake up with a heavy heart and honestly in a bit of a fright
I've come face to face with more than just my own demons tonight

The pain of the earth is so much more than mine will ever be
I'm overwhelmed with this burden, like it was just handed to me

Suddenly, I feel the wounds of the world in this strange toxicity
The abrasions are on me now and they're mine to forever carry

The cracks on the seabed reflect the cracks on my skin
The world is broken, I am open, it's time to let the light in

I don't know what to live for anymore, it feels hopeless
I won't let myself spiral out again, I need to stay focused

Keep myself on track, I just have even more to fight for
Spread my love beyond all the hatred, a joy ambassador

Remembering who I am and trusting I am destined to win
Golden lenses back on, I know I'm here to be a champion

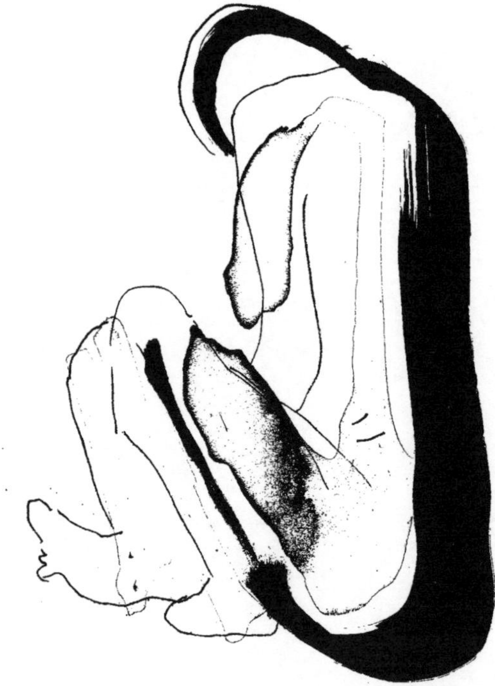

MASK UNVEILED

Somehow in the seas I have felt our deepest tragedy
Grieving this time, not for me, but for humanity

I've been swimming reluctantly through our vague history
Carefully trying to untangle this confusing toxic mystery

Humans greedily tearing apart this naturally abundant planet
Just because tricky villains put money in our empty pocket

We are all one with the universe, our energies create this version of reality
Gluttonous rulers in control, our precious land in catastrophe

The quicker we heal, the quicker we can restore mother earth
She's begging for us to wake, to care for our perishing hearth

Repeating mistakes and walking in our comfortable sleep
We are nothing but a herd of oblivious blind sheep

From society's problems to still trying to solve my own
Holding the weight of the world and I feel incredibly alone

A renewed sense of purpose, a part of me I'm supposed to be
Searching for that girl living in those golden orbs down in the barren sea

This is much bigger than me and the game I've been playing
Hey, Monster, is that what you have been saying?

I have seen more than enough and now I feel so helpless
This dazed society we're in is starting to feel so useless

One by one, I'm flexing my back and pulling out the swords
How do I put all of this outrageous nonsense into words?

Another sunset, another solemn day says goodbye
Pastel pink clouds like dripping sand castles through the sky

Full moon burns so bright, I absorb her into my third eye
Straight cord to the moon, our own telephone wire

Tossing and turning, wide awake, I check the clock, it's 11:11
Insomnia, 2:22, 3:33 on the dot, it must be divine intervention

I need to breathe slowly, stay calm, and find the white light
I can't avoid my shit because that's what keeps me up at night

I wonder who I would be if that night when I was twelve never happened?
Is pain part of my path, am I meant to live a life so saddened?

I'm still waiting for something to unlock, where is my key?
Searching for a sign in all these symbols and synchronicity

I thought I was close to figuring all this stuff out
But this monster is still lurking in me, it won't let me forget

Hey Monster, one question I never had the courage to ask
Who are you underneath that fucking grotesque mask?

It's like the second I inquire, my little body begins to retire
My energy is shifting and I can feel it spark and rewire

I get it now, you want to be free, you don't want to cause pain
You're stronger than me, maybe it's time that I let you reign

Carefully peeling the mask, I look at you, you see me and smile
Wait, has it been the real me all along, my fucking inner child?

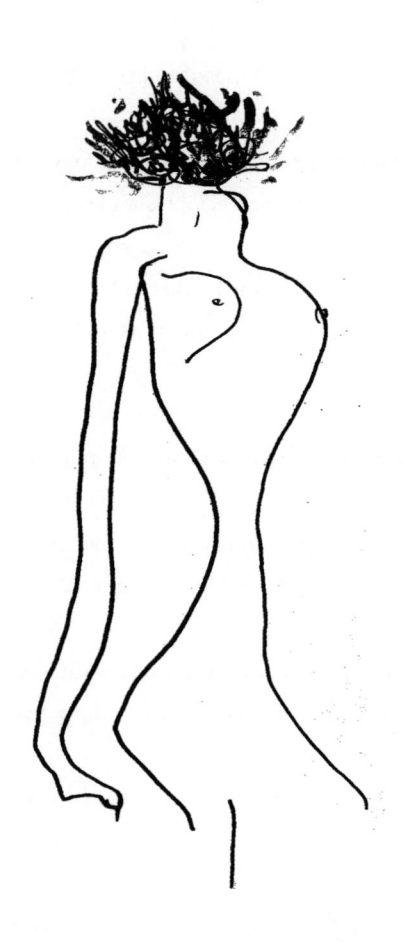

TRANSCENDENCE

Blanket of gray, clouds of sympathy and grief woven in the sky
My teardrops ascend into heaven and together we cry

I take a deep breath and light my white jasmine candles
999 Hz on and I'm reaching out to all my nearest angels

I break my red lenses, ground myself, and balance my root
I've come home to myself and can stand on my steady foot

Laying in African marigolds and I release all my control
Honoring my sacred womb and trusting my own inner sacral

Finally exuding confidence as I am closer to my soul purpose
I pour yellow sunshine into my slowly healing solar plexus

Emerald and jade laying on my chest to rebalance my heart
Secret green clues from before, I sensed from the start

A hint of pungent peppermint oil wafting from my throat
I am courageous, I am brave, I will always speak my truth

The indigo winds whisper and my third eye tingles
I am beginning to listen to my tiny little forehead tickles

Amethysts and angelites decorating my royal crown
Flying into the violet light, I'm not coming back down

Trading my mirrored gravestones for sparkling gemstones
Mending my deeply rooted wounds and fractured bones

Curious, I slice into the veil with my reclaimed silver sword
I get a quick glimpse into a vaguely familiar world

Blurring the lines between my dreams and actuality
Messages, visions, I'm trying to keep my lucidity

I have begun to love traveling through the celestial
Escaping to the stars and playing in the extraterrestrial

Universe within universe, none of this matters, huh?
I zoom out and take another look, oh, I think nah

Bright white light as I'm staring into all the galaxies
I can suddenly feel the truth behind all the fallacies

I thought therapy would help me, but I need something more
There's too much going on in my mind for me to ignore

The weight of being a child of immigrants, the pressures of cultures clashing
The weight of this cosmic abyss in me that only keeps expanding

I'm not sure that anyone else is able to help me get better
I want to find my red thread and weave all the pieces together

Flashbacks from my young past and I know it's not my first time in space
Did I halt my own journey to protect what my teenage self could no longer brace?

Have I always been this galactic sort of way, did I block my growth again?
I buried my key to the skies down in the seas with no traces of a recovery plan

What is the point of existence?
I am diving way too deep into this

I think I just opened my mind to something I can't explain
I'm feeling way too much at once, am I going insane?

Hey, come back to the present, there's no need to overthink
There's no need to be lost, just slow down and stay in sync

I feel so deeply and I'm so damn sensitive
Maybe someday this will give me empathetic perspective

INNER CHILD SPEAKS

I feel like a piece of candy inside your old birthday pinata
Watching an overrated show at the overpriced cinema

Deciphering hieroglyphics since twelve years of age
I've been naturally ripening into a wise hierophant sage

Back then, I was so afraid of being alone and abandoned
I betrayed myself instead, now that I've been enlightened

I hid myself away and let things get off track and messy
I was too scared to stay, please show me some mercy

Outer forces were too forceful and looped us on repeat
Finally awakened and we are no longer dazed to deceit

You took care of us, thank you for getting us this far
But I've been training for this, now I am a warrior

I'm still here and I have not given up on you
Just let me come out, I can fight this through

I can't let you go on, we need to realign to our divine path
There's so much more for us than life in this aftermath

You are so worthy, I have loved you all along
You sang for me and I listened to every song

I know you could never feel my love, or the love of anyone else
I've been sending you spirit animals and ringing all the
internal bells

I've been scratching at the edges of your interior walls
Peeling off outdated wallpaper and releasing my shackles

Slicing away at the layers of your mind, like peeling film
out of a camera
So many secrets hidden in these reels, like an old historic drama

Love, fear, joy, pain, so much goes into being alive
Feeling is living, living is feeling, and you deserve to thrive

So, please don't be scared of the pain, just feel the damn feeling
This is why we are here, this is why I have been screaming

You've gotten so far on your own despite feeling abandoned
It's up to you to open up and let the all the love in

Hanging onto the pain makes it bigger and bigger
Just let some go each time you feel a little trigger

It's hard to accept that this is no longer who you are
The wounds may always stay, I'll always be your scar

It's time for something new, this extended grieving cycle is closing
It's time to be true now, this assumed identity you are outgrowing

The magic has been here since the beginning of time
I've been protecting the key until you reached your prime

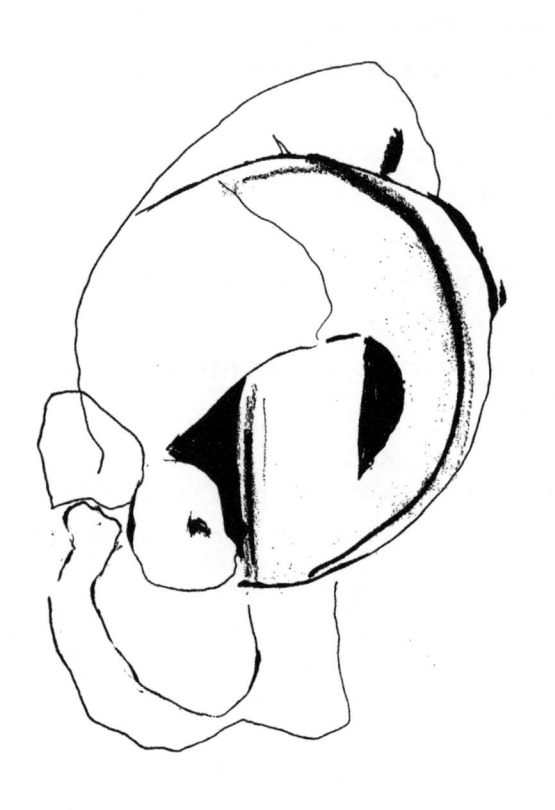

REBIRTH

The biggest wake up call, all of a sudden I understand my
damage
I finally turn my survival mode off and I have plenty left to
salvage

The doll in me, this monster in me comes to life with a start
I'm a whole movie with plot twists and turns, I'm a work of art

Maybe I do need to let go and die, I don't have to die a
physical death
Make space for this new me, a chance to take a fresh
mental breath

No wonder I have felt like dying, I really have been dying
Between my ego and fears, old parts of me are perishing

From a small grit of pain, I began creating my pretty pearl
Beauty in the ugliness and I'm breaking my oyster shell

I feel like I just stepped into my own skin
I have finally synced up and I am sovereign

A victim no more, I let go and release some more sorrow
I'm very grateful for this chance to see a pretty morrow

Damaged girl in a harsh world and I let myself conform
Not scared anymore, at last, I have weathered this storm

Saying goodbye to the abuse, my old self, and to society's rules
They no longer define me, they are just my sharpened tools

Guardians and guides along for the ride, a team of spiritual passengers
Sending clues from the skies and through magical animal messengers

Guiding me, my inner self, my higher self has been here all along
Writing me back to my dream world, to which I rightfully belong

I always been worthy, I'd say I deserve even more than I can imagine
I'm already taking a step towards the unknown, a new path I have chosen

Show myself the same grace that I always extend to others
So much love to come hidden in these next new chapters

A whole human adventure of experiencing all the emotions
Practicing self-awareness, staying centered, and making steady decisions

A bit unsure, I'm trying so hard not to feel like an imposter
It's time to rewrite this score, now I am the new composer

Divine timing as I align, my kismet written in the stars
Confirmations from above, the world showing up in my cards

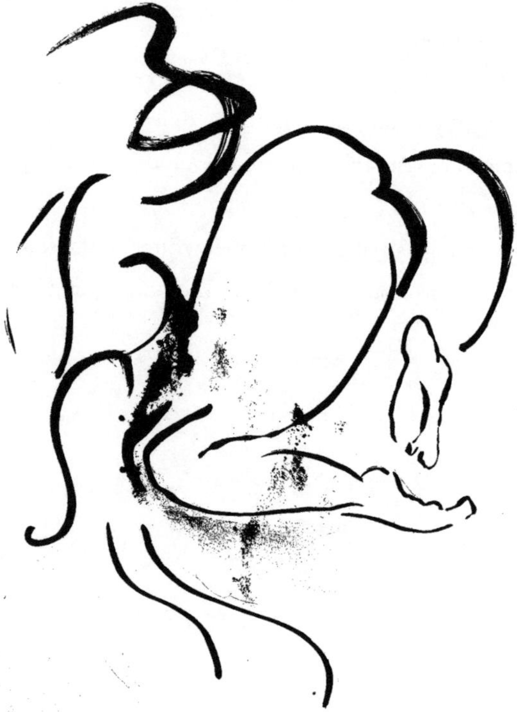

METAMORPHOSIS

Close my eyes and dive into the sea once more
My fish are there looking damaged from this war

Grown a bit of meat on their fragile bones, yet they look unwell
Translucent, frail, and pale, sadly still cast under my old spell

A reminder of my wounds, they are unknowingly taunting
Yet blameless, they are frightened and also frightening

At one with myself now and I know I have the power to heal
From the inside out, it's my own internal force to feel

I pour moonlight out from within and create a new golden orb
Reiki magic in my hands, they transform as they begin to absorb

Plumping up, saturating up, golden yellow fire in their eyes
Gilded dragons of once deadly waters, they alchemize

Remembering who I am in the depths of the sea
Shining my recharged light and shifting the energy

Grateful for my strong bones, my tough skin, and my courage
Grateful for my strength, my journey, and my right to passage

Forgiving my winters for lasting longer than they should
Harnessing my powers, I can use them for greater good

Forgiving my parents for not knowing any better in uncertain times
Showing them grace, no longer punishing them for their innocent crimes

Forgiving my old self for making mistakes under all the pressure
Navigating abuse, adulthood, only to uncover my own treasure

Forgiving God/Universe, remembering we all have free will
Staying true to myself and following my gut is my best skill

Forgiving myself for rejecting myself and my culture
Learning to have pride in my own unique mixture

Red threads from my hip hop days, black eyeliner from my emo nights
An homage to all my old selves, now they glow under the limelights

I'm sewn together like a patchwork of quilted history
All the ripped up ugly pictures now part of my beauty

A sense of understanding, the puzzle is getting clearer
Just a scene from my past, or maybe even from my future

Peace is overwhelming, joy is flowing
My lips are smiling, waxing moon is glowing

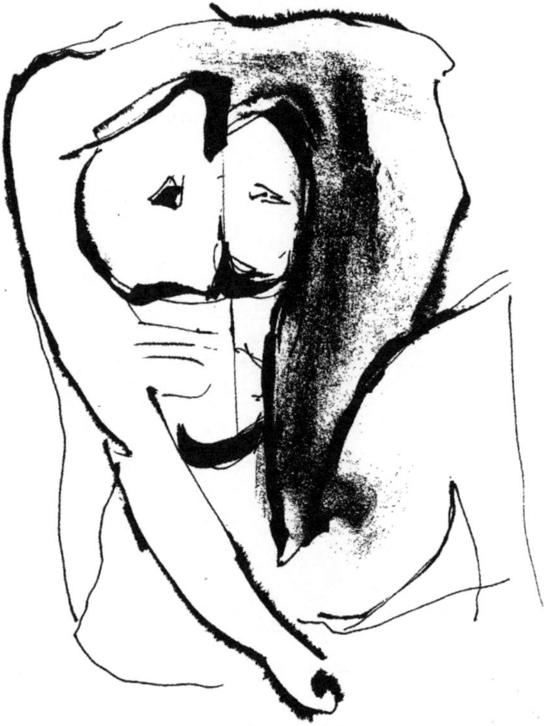

HIGH PRIESTESS

Time to sleep and I have a new bedtime ritual to get ready
I'm in the kitchen warming milk with turmeric and honey

I catch motion outside and see these glowing green eyes
A sweet black cat stares at me, is that you, goddess Isis?

A delicate white feather flutters down like a signal
Watching from heaven, my sweet guardian angel

The sun and the moon, their love clandestine
Like Yin and Yang, masculine and feminine

The moon and the ocean tides are so obviously connected
Hey, Mars and Venus, what else is being affected?

From a wild werewolf so unknowingly triggered
To enlightened by the moon, in sync and empowered

I bleed when the moon is full, it's kind of divine
To feel interconnected and so very much aligned

To think that once I felt I had no place in this world
I would have missed out on all this boundless love

Honoring my natural cycles of rest and play
No longer feeling guilty when I want to just lay

Letting structures fall and it turns out I love to be feminine
Smudging my harsh lines, slowly my outer edges soften

I turn on the water and squeeze eucalyptus in the shower
Upbeat music blasting loudly to teleport me for an hour

I can close my eyes and let go and get lost in the moment
Temporary escape and I can feel freely in the movement

I pour fresh rice milk in my hair in an evanescent cascade
Scorching off my chest like I'm an old fashioned milkmaid

Dripping beads like a moonstone skirt on my body
Swaying off my hips, I am at my own dance party

Bringing my hands together in cho ku ray
I am the goddess of fire, my reiki chant I say

I'm dancing around with an aura of golden radiance
Playing with the ethereal like I'm a damn enchantress

Massaging coconut oil into my soft supple caramel skin
Textured like crushed nutmeg and brown sugar cinnamon

I want to be that girl from my dreams, I want to heal for good this time
The darkness is a part of me, but even the moon needs the sun to shine

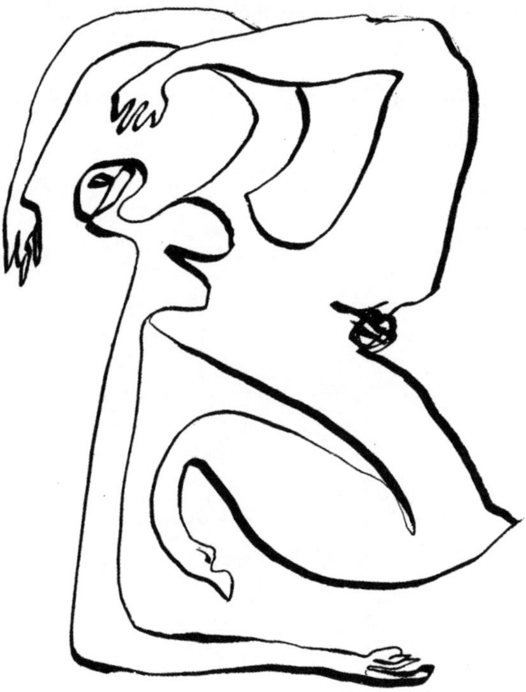

MAGICIAN

I wake up happy to be alive, and greet the sun like a swan
While I whisper my daily gratitude in my lemon tea at dawn

I've been opening my heart and recalibrating my compass
Trusting my intuition, living in my truth is my only purpose

From the east to the west, I'm taking an architectural section
Beyond the horizons, I'm looking for some kind of direction

There's a fire burning in me as I gather my shined instruments
Air, earth, and sea, I'm powered by all the natural elements

Standing on the edge again, glancing into the unknown at what I fear
I can see on the other side of this, what I want is right there

I've seen my trauma, accepted, and released my anger
I think the hardest part is over, I just have to stay aware

But my home, family, friends, job, something is still wrong
I feel like it's time to move on, I still feel like I don't belong

Hanging onto the cracks of my split past, I'm slipping away
I'm holding onto my old life, I don't think I'm meant to stay

I wonder why I have been chosen to endure all these painful battles?
Is this just part of being human, conquering our own struggles?

My sweet cardinal Ruby finds himself a partner already
A message of love in my garden, I'm calling her Lady
Otherworldly unknown, are you just myths and legends?
I'll never really know, but you're still full of potent lessons

What does it all mean, and why does it matter?
Is there something more or is it just poetic glamor?

I quiet my thoughts and dig into my concealed wisdom
An infinite source of cloaked mastery that's yet to become

No matter what the truth is, I have released my own curse
No longer misguided and I trust my mysterious universe

Tearing down the limestones off my home, exposing my
inner soul with pride
Putting my delicate heart on the market and I know I'm
gorgeous inside

My vibes are high, I burn bay leaves and patchouli incense
I feel like I'm protected by my magical white picket fence

Watching the smoke spin like ghosts dancing in a slow spiral
I close my eyes, lift and stare openly beyond the thinly knit veil

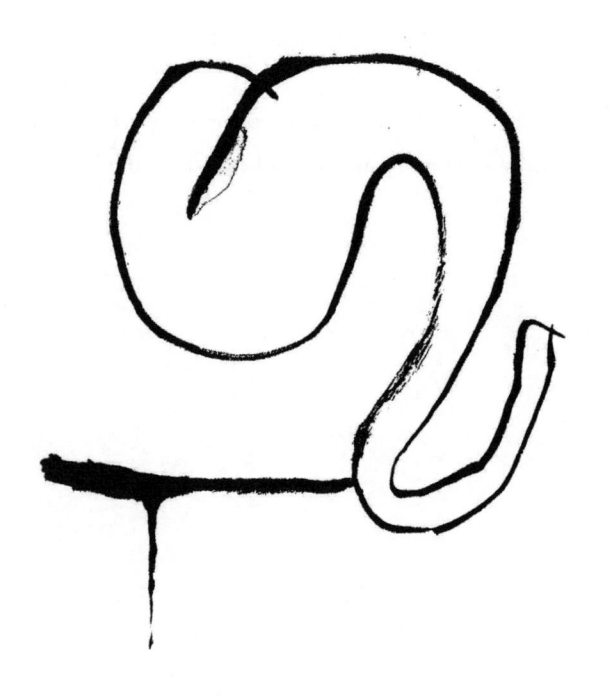

SEA DRAGONS

Another long winter passes and I welcome the spring
Close my eyes and go to see how my dragons are progressing

963 Hz on and I can already feel the waves of the sound bath
Swimming to the bottom and I look down for the unfolding path

I see tiny glimmers of light in the midnight blue sea
Golden specks in the depths made of lapis lazuli

Swimming to me wearing halos on their heads like lanterns
Sparkling drops of stars shooting out of underwater caverns

They all come together and refract the moon like a chandelier
Once ghastly candlelight, now lighting the sea, so cavalier

Covered in scales like slices of citrine and tiger's eye
Am I deep down in the sea or up high in the starry night sky?

They remind me of pretty mosaic tiles I use in my designs
Perfect patterns in my dreams, no need for straight lines

No longer scary, but strangely angelic now, and fierce
Dragons of the sea swimming in their newfound peace

Those old pains of mine are now shined tools on my belt
They are the specks in my gemstones and the gold that I melt

The dullness can only sparkle after putting in the work to cleanse
I've stared the devil in his eyes and saw myself in his red lens

I am healing my body, I am healthy, I am so beautiful
I feel alive from my healing insides, from my reviving soul

Releasing the trauma stored in my body, my mind is my own medicine
I have found my place on this planet and am no longer my own assassin

Understanding how my body is linked to my triggers
No more migraines, stomachaches, no more night terrors

Mirroring my thoughts, my subconscious creates my reality
Fish and feathers in my visions, the universe always guides me

Moonlight in the dark night, alarm bells in my quiet mind
I can see you, I can hear you, I know the rest will unwind

My brave sea dragons welcome me to my calmed waters
My emotions run smooth, I've unmasked all my monsters

My intuition knows the way through this wild unknown
I follow my dragons as they lead me to my hidden throne

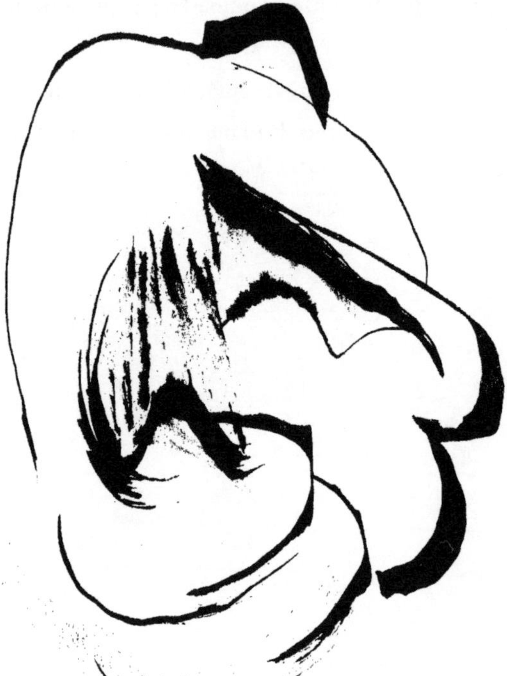

DEVIL IN RED SNAKESKIN

Garnet and bloodstone encrusted on my sensual body
Lying here in the waning crescent moon, all sparkly

I close my eyes one more time and begin to meditate
Wandering in the violet light, back to my serene state

I'm hanging like a serpent, my one redeeming string
My chakras align, is this a Kundalini awakening?

Rising from my root all the way to my crown
Feeling like Medusa in this ruby studded ball gown

Madness within me yet I'm grounded from my base
Instead of killing me my snake has held me in place

I can feel the release of the grip of the snake
My neck is now free and it forces me awake

I never thought your poisonous apple would be my elixir
Unlocking secret codes with my powerful decrypter

Not scared of snakes, now they're my weapons to yield
Transmuting pain into power, my skin is my armor and shield

Shame and guilt are not my lifetime burdens to bear
They're your crimes and giving them to me is unfair

Meeting me was the best thing that ever happened to you
A demon with two faces, you thought I had no clue

I may have made your life interesting for a moment
But you ruined my life without even thinking about it

You're the nicest guy, so sufficiently charming
You've got everyone fooled, it's very alarming
With your sly smile, you preyed on my innocence
Your karma will return, I am praying for vengeance

I know what everyone will tell me to help lighten my blue
I've forgiven myself and I don't think I need to forgive you

You took away my purity, my value, my safety net in my home
You left me worthless, broken, living an unpainted life in monochrome

Using my discernment and authorizing my own immaculacy
Head held high, unchaining myself from institutional lunacy

I'm not a victim playing defense, I'm prowling for you on the offense
I've harnessed my flames, I have become the queen of darkness

Black lace choker on my neck, now an accessory to murder
That old me is dead and gone and it's unnecessary to miss her

Silky raven feathered wings strung with beads of onyx
My horns are ready to come out on the next lunar eclipse

Climbing my thighs my boot heels high, stitched of red snakeskin
Dancing on Neptune, black outer space sky, it's raining diamonds

I'm not hiding in the shadows, it's witching hour and I soar in the night
A queen of wands burning through eternal fire and am I my own light

Broken mirrors on my chest so you can see your own flaws
I'm a ray of sunshine, but I'll burn you if you get too close

I'll cut you out with my sword and you know I'll never look back
Boundaries of steel reinforcing me and keeping me on track

I am the devil, I am the monster, I am fearless, and I want you to see me
Empowered by anger and rage, I am everything you could never be

I wield the might of the seas with the help of Poseidon
You deserve all the venom that drips from the fangs of my trident

There's still a golden halo on my head, don't get me wrong
But don't you cross me, I've been the dark angel all along

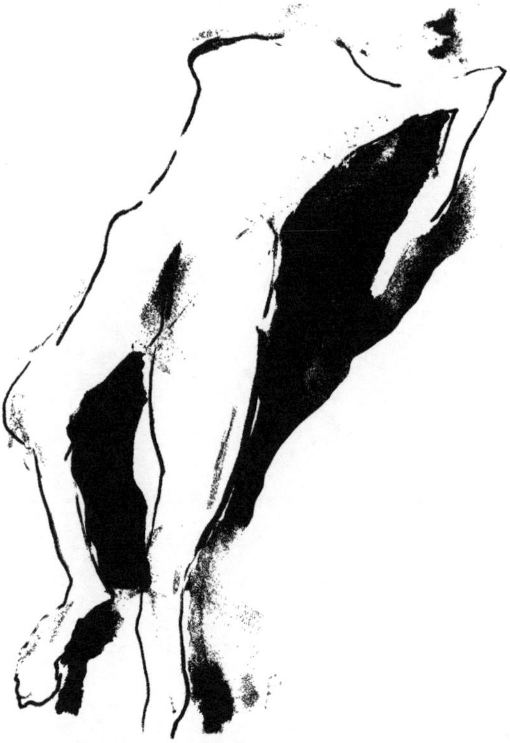

EMPEROR IN REVERSE

Snap back into the existence of the old me, my old identity
Corporate job, busy schedule, doesn't align with the new me

My once dominating masculine energy begins to harmonize
Repressed feminine is awakened and needs to synthesize

401K, average health benefits, not a terrible salary
Deep inside though this could be the true death of me

Student loans, mortgage, gas, and a car bill
Advised to be in this system, yet it feels like a trap still

They make a really pretty glass box these days
Great views, yummy snacks, and sometimes a decent raise

The higher I climb this ladder, the less I feel like me
Just a good girl being an even better employee

I'm starting to wonder how humans even fit into this picture?
Caught in the seaweeds, the story must be bigger

Check all the boxes and just fill the role
Employee 1,2,3 and I'm easily replaceable

Over and over, recreating the same scene
Different directors, the same movie to be seen

Who is telling the story, is there only one stage?
Is there a different tale on the next page?

I'm back to being a puppet in society's game
Cut me free, I don't want to be tame

Working to live, no home without income
Born to be a slave to this toxic system

Maybe capitalism is a delirium filled with bribes
Stuck us on repeat and banking on our low vibes

I've loved being a designer, building schools for a living
But something is off, maybe something is missing

This education system seems to be getting outdated
Jobs are disappearing and soon will be automated

Training kids to be trapped in this program
Why are some of us born to fail this exam?

I want no part in this plan, this old way feels misled
Kids are new energy, they should teach us instead

I feel sick to my stomach learning about school safety design
New products coming out with gun shelter in mind

Automatic doors, safety glass, gates for security
Temporary solutions, we are a fucked up society

Keeping visibility in mind when planning classroom layouts
Swapping glass for casework to hide behind in case of any shootouts

Can't even design open courtyards for kids to run free
This is not how I want life for my future children to be

I feel so wrong, so useless, building a bulletproof prison
It's like saying "yes" and giving shooters full permission

Are we really doing the best that we can?
Gun violence can't be on a designer's hands

Hurt people hurt people and breed fears and anxiety
What about mental health and healing the community?

Unbalanced masculine energies running this sloppy show
Outdated system controlled by the aggressive male ego

Black moon Lilith liberating me from the wounded patriarchy
Soft can be strong, we should not be treated inadequately

I've called back my femininity that I buried so long ago
Dominating masculine energy doesn't resonate or flow

I can't keep committing to a life that doesn't feel right
I never wanted to go this way, I never trusted my light

This isn't where I'm supposed to be, I don't belong here
I need space to figure out myself, I need time to breathe

I'm so disconnected and I feel completely out of place
There has got to be a way out of this senseless rat race

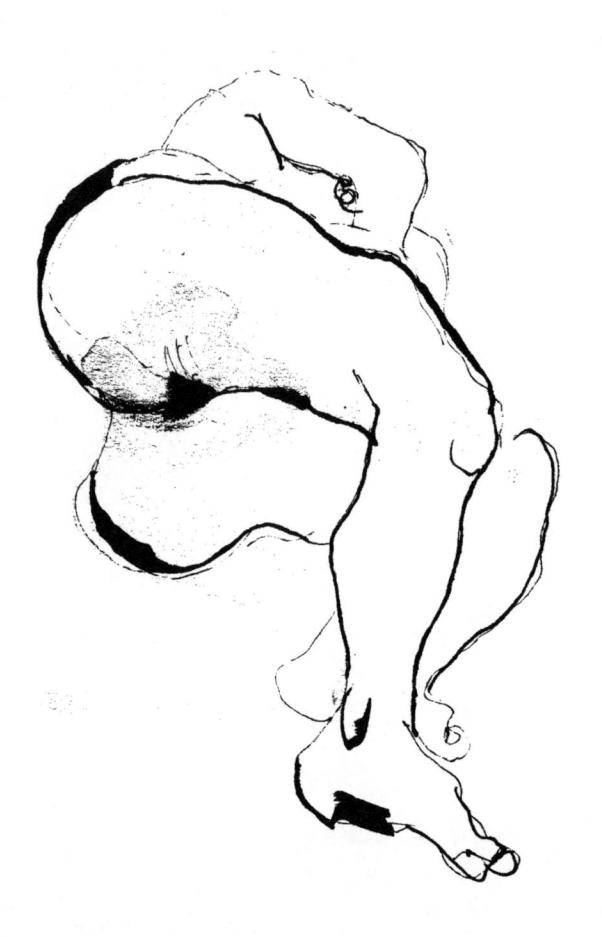

EMPRESS STATE OF MIND

My creativity isn't on demand and I'm tapping out
What once felt right is now clouded with doubt

I am tired of living in this false sense of surety
When will the scales of justice weigh in for me?

Honeybee flies by and reminds me of my sweet fertility
A sign from above, I can create a new version of reality

I choose to live out my own destiny, I have free will to
play my hand
I am no longer afraid to take a chance, I am going all in

I am the opposite of who society keeps trying to train me to be
I don't care about this stiff uniform or my capping out salary

The known has become more scary than the unknown
I crave to learn more, I feel a new path is being shown

I hate that I've turned into an indoor creature
I want to go out there, I want to be in nature

Planted like a tree and my feet bare in the grass
Growing taller out here, there are no ceilings of glass

My game, my rules, this is my experiment
Rewards and pleasure, I'm gonna make it worth it

If I lose, then I lose, but I get a new hand to play
Can't sit here and fold, living the same life in replay

It's scary as hell to walk away with no idea of what's next
Yet, sticking around for this mess would be failing this test

So close to the top, but I'm ready to jump off this ladder
Burn it down behind me like it like it doesn't even matter

I walk away from my job and my house of cards crumbles
I'm not scared of losing, I'm not scared of taking tumbles

Exit stage left, I look back and see you and all your puppet strings
The show must go on, I watch as you jump through the rings

I thank my old life, my blessings, my privileges, and my position
I am grateful for the success thus far to afford me this new exploration

I am changing my views by changing out my lens
Same place, new me, and I can see new horizons

My anger, pain, and sorrows have been way too heavy
I'm finally letting them go and now I can breathe easy

Every new trigger highlighting every old point of pain
Keep cleaning out the wounds and let the lessons remain

Pulling the roots from within my solar plexus
Spinning weeds into golden wheat like I'm an empress

I don't want to hide, I don't want to be a chameleon
I'm going to break free, I'm going to make a million

Maybe there's an ace of wands coming my way
So, I'm going to spark my match and light my flame

I am the queen of swords and I can finally slash though this old life
Long time coming, I'm taking a calculated risk with my pretty turquoise knife

No more creating my own bad luck, no more fear
There's plenty to go around and I'll take my share

Fortune favors the bold, I am my own heroic savior
My balance is paid, may the odds ever be in my favor

I have to play the game to win and I know I will come out on top
Lightning, thunder, big storms start with just a tiny raindrop

Rubies filled with secrets in my grenadine fountain
Bathing for my 32nd birthday in my pomegranate potion

The end of my longest year ever is here at last
Maybe, just maybe, I can finally release my past

Once I'm in, once I'm hot, luck is on my side
What a gift this July, I'm in an empress state of mind

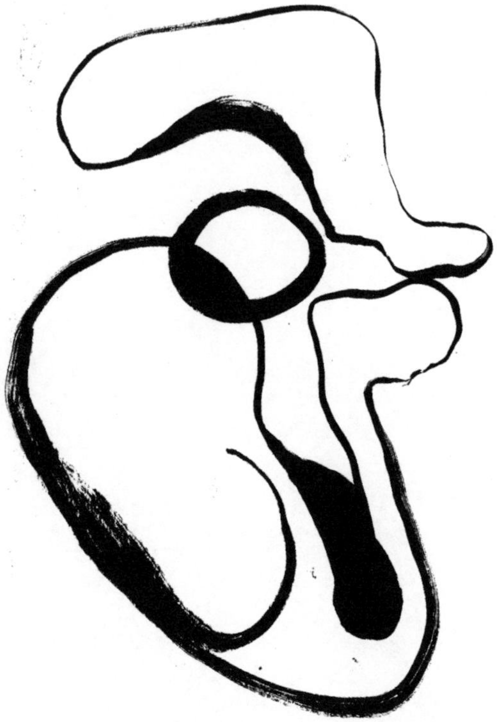

PEARL GIRL

I am now in the deepest part of the sea
Cold as ice and my dragons aren't around me

The water is blacker than ever, yet it feels clean
The murkiness has settled and so has my vision

The sea may be cold, but I have flames for wings
They keep me warm, alive, and forever gleaming

Moonlight glowing from within me like an aura of pearl
My inner white light, I am home in my own safety bubble

I look down at my strengthened cinnamon skin
Like my dragons, I am made of scales of deep citrine

Shards of broken silver swords forged into my breastplate and pauldron
Diamonds on my gauntlets, I'm an alchemical magic cauldron

Angelite and larimar woven together like a tapestry
I am made of the sea as she reflects onto me

A fire mermaid softened by the Dirac sea
Fire and ice, together in perfect harmony

Wearing my wounds with pride like shiny stars
No longer ashamed to show you my battle scars

You see me but you see you when you see me
The pretty, the bad, the starlight, even the ugly

I am your mirror, I speak in riddles and scribe like an oracle
A pearlescent spirit, I see that I am magnificently mystical

A splatter of oil, a holographic rainbow in the chasm
A black hole in the sea, an iridescent red-lipped phantom

Diving deeper, shining my light onto shadows
Innocent and free, I've destroyed my own gallows

Just swimming in the infinite, grounded to the cosmos
Magnetically tethered to the core of the universe

My little golden sea dragons have finally found me
It's my turn to lead and they follow me trustingly

We sprinkle our golden moondust onto the seafloor
Lighting the path for those behind me to come explore

Something tiny shimmers in the powdery sand up ahead
I swim a bit closer and make my way down to the seabed

It's a teardrop of a golden Ankh, I pull out my old memento
The key of nourishing life, of wisdom that I buried so long ago

A feeling of deja vu, I wonder what kind of new beginning awaits
The perfumed fragrance of abundance of my heart emanates

I am of the planet, of the seas, of the sun, and of the skies, I am an aligned compass
I am of earth, of water, of fire, and of air, I am of the elements of the universe

Destiny versus free will, I still have so many questions
At the helm of my fate now and I'm open to suggestions

I crave new people in new places with new chances at
compassionate love
It's time to swim out of this sea and fly away free like a
humbled dove

To all the haunting ghosts of my past who may feel strange
I accept and forgive without expecting anything to change

Two little fireflies buzzing under the dusky moonrise
Promises prancing in my eyes with a bittersweet sacrifice

Synchronicities in my path, my only external validation
Releasing all my chains without any more apprehension

I'm chasing after that girl running in the starry meadows
I can't wait to see her, to be her, I feel like I'm so close

My throne in the skies on the moon, I was there all along
My jewels glow in the sun, I always am right where I belong

Keep going, keep fighting, I make myself this promise
I have only just begun this rebirth as a moon goddess

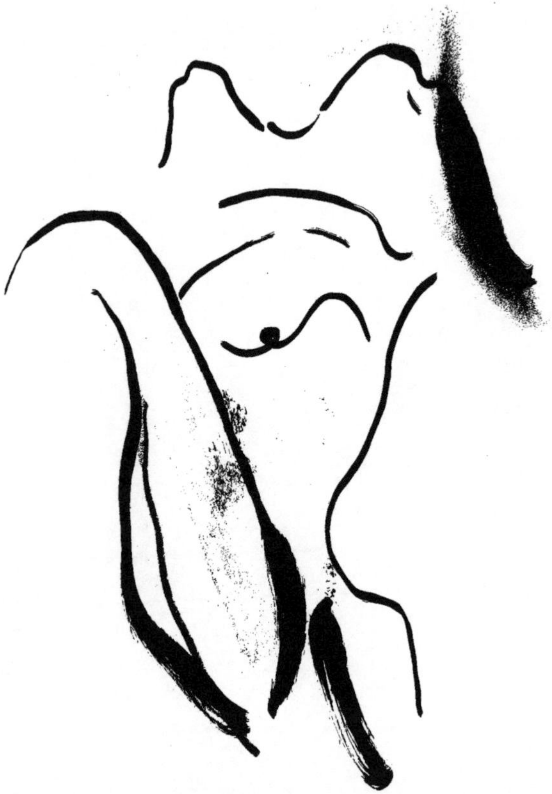

GOLDEN HOUR

Head back in space, I'm hopping off Saturn's beige rings
Flying to Jupiter, I can feel my luck is actually turning

At the center of it all, there's nothing but whiteness
Filled with the light, I'm staring at my blank canvas

No longer cozy, I've happily left my comfort zone
Pushing my boundaries and I'm going it alone

To feel is to live and I want slow and savory
I am ready to embark on my grandest safari

Not chasing anything, it's my heart I'm following
It'll make sense one day, all in divine timing

Daydreams and nightmares, I harness the beauty of the darkness
I will always be your strength, but you will never be my weakness

Just enough sorrow to churn from my soul
Pouring an ombre light, truth written in the scroll

The universe is judging and clearing my karma today
Wheel of fortune turns as the stars align on my way

I have the power to change my own life
Maybe even sway the direction of my afterlife

Paradise on earth and I have the golden ticket
I'm cleared for takeoff, will the other side be worth it?

Standing at the gate with my ticket on my phone
Just like in my dream, but this time I'm not alone

Lots of people around me and this is really happening
No looking back now, my whole future is remapping

I walk down the aisle and stare at my reflection in the window
I'm staring back at myself, here and now, and in my own glow

I look at myself and watch the tears fall from my eyes
Happy, nervous, excited, and I'm filled with butterflies

My plane takes off into the dusk, this is my golden hour
Scared and owning it, I'm still flying steadily in my power

I tingle with excitement as I set off on this solo adventure
I can't wait to discover what's written in my next chapter

No plans, no goals, letting the universe drive this time
I've released all control and I trust I'll find what's mine

The world is mine, the more I learn, the less I know
A humbling of my mind, let the wisdom come in and flow

I am the wildflower girl in the meadows, I am finally here
I am here to dance freely, and I am free to be the real me

Trusting the divine that I have balanced my karma
It's about damn time to set the sun on my trauma